T0384455

ATTRACT
RETAIN
&
DEVELOP

Shaping a Skilled
Workforce for the Future

ATTRACT

RETAIN

&

DEVELOP

NICHOLAS WYMAN

FC

**FAST
COMPANY**
Press

This publication is designed to provide accurate and authoritative information in regard to the subject matter covered. It is sold with the understanding that the publisher and author are not engaged in rendering legal, accounting, or other professional services. Nothing herein shall create an attorney–client relationship, and nothing herein shall constitute legal advice or a solicitation to offer legal advice. If legal advice or other expert assistance is required, the services of a competent professional should be sought.

Fast Company Press
New York, New York
www.fastcompanypress.com

Copyright © 2025 Nicholas Wyman

All rights reserved.

Thank you for purchasing an authorized edition of this book and for complying with copyright law. No part of this book may be reproduced, stored in a retrieval system, or transmitted by any means, electronic, mechanical, photocopying, recording, or otherwise, without written permission from the copyright holder.

This work is being published under the Fast Company Press imprint by an exclusive arrangement with *Fast Company*. *Fast Company* and the *Fast Company* logo are registered trademarks of Mansueto Ventures, LLC. The Fast Company Press logo is a wholly owned trademark of Mansueto Ventures, LLC.

Distributed by Greenleaf Book Group

For ordering information or special discounts for bulk purchases, please contact Greenleaf Book Group at PO Box 91869, Austin, TX 78709, 512.891.6100.

Design and composition by Greenleaf Book Group and Teresa Muniz
Cover design by Greenleaf Book Group and Teresa Muniz
Cover images used under license from ©Adobe Stock/efks.
Concorde image used under license from ©GettyImages/Buzzpictures.

Publisher's Cataloging-in-Publication data is available.

Print ISBN: 978-1-63908-121-9

eBook ISBN: 978-1-63908-122-6

To offset the number of trees consumed in the printing of our books, Greenleaf donates a portion of the proceeds from each printing to the Arbor Day Foundation. Greenleaf Book Group has replaced over 50,000 trees since 2007.

Printed in the United States of America on acid-free paper

25 26 27 28 29 30 31   10 9 8 7 6 5 4 3 2 1

First Edition

Contents

———

PART IV: CONNECT

CONCLUSION: THE LAST BITE 245

The Path Less Traveled

OVER THE DECADES, MY JOURNEY HAS TAKEN ME FROM being an award-winning chef to leading the international Institute for Workplace Skills and Innovation (IWSI), where I've built up expertise in job skills training. Our group employs eight hundred apprentices at any given time and has successfully graduated more than 20,000 others. We have a network of more than three hundred small, medium, and large employer partners.

Although I hung up my apron a few years back, I still keep in touch with my culinary roots. My philosophy today leans toward farm-to-table, focusing on organic, locally sourced ingredients, and I try to live a lifestyle that's clean and healthy.

My goal here has been to not create yet another "formula" book on the workings of the workplace. And just to be up-front, I'm no McKinsey-style management guide. You won't find robotic, data-driven analysis or structured methodologies here. What you *will* find are practical ideas, including some key ingredients such as mentoring, mastering change in a tech-driven world, and building a resilient, innovative workforce culture. To this I have mixed in (hopefully) some entrepreneurial hustle (the same hustle that gets startups off the ground).

This book is a culmination of my diverse (some say crazy) background. From culinary to corporate, talent development to embracing change, my aim is to offer fresh insights into the workplace. Those insights often take a different track from the age-old "get into a good college" mentality. Not that I have anything against college students. It's just that in the modern age, there are many options to consider. As a hiring manager or business owner, you need to have a keen awareness of who's out there seeking employment and what they can offer your team. You need to know how you will captivate them and demonstrate why you want them on your team—and how you will entice them to stick around for a while.

Join me on a journey as we explore innovative strategies, redefining the future of work. The path for which I advocate is a path less traveled, but one rich with creative solutions and ideas that can lead to impactful change.

Acknowledgments

———

THIS BOOK WOULD NOT HAVE BEEN POSSIBLE WITHOUT the invaluable support and guidance of many. I extend my deepest gratitude to editor Rich Mintzer. Thanks to all the individuals mentioned throughout this book—your contributions have shaped this journey in countless ways.

To my wife, Prue, and my children, James and Alexandra (Alex), your love and support are my greatest treasures. The joy and encouragement you bring into my life have been my foundation, and I am profoundly grateful for the happiness we share as a family.

Thank you to Dr. Deborah Williamson and her skilled team for their indispensable efforts.

A big thanks to Frederick (Fred) Maddern, O.B.E., who formulated the Levin Plan, which led me to move to North America. Thanks to Patti Dirlam for always thinking one step ahead, and to Nat Brambilla for keeping me connected to what matters most: advancing opportunities for young people. Special thanks to Sophie Ramsey, James (Jim) Lawrence, Dr. Robert (Bob) Lerman, Stuart Newman, Professor Steve Hamilton, Zach Boren, John Dunn, Michael Bernick, Cynthia Walker, Commander Bill Kraus (USN-Ret), Felix Veski, Jordan Walley, Margaret Paton, and the "intentional warriors" for keeping me grounded and focused.

Each of you has played a pivotal role in this endeavor, and I am profoundly thankful.

Introduction

––––

THE FUTURE WON'T WAIT, AND NEITHER SHOULD YOUR company. So what's holding you back?

In a recent report by the World Economic Forum, an astonishing 44 percent of workers' skills are expected to change within the next five years.[1] Adding to this transformative landscape, more than 85 percent of companies are bracing for a tech-driven transformation, marking a shift in how their businesses will have to operate.

Skill transformation in the workforce is not just knocking at the door—it's barging on in. This shift underlines the urgency for many companies to change with the times and the need for a fresh approach to workforce development.

Amidst a backdrop of strained global supply chains and economic uncertainty, the need for resilience and adaptability in businesses has never been more critical. Companies, now more than ever, need to Get Shit Done (#GSD). They need to balance the chaos of economic shifts with the aspirations of their workforce for meaningful work and work–life harmony.

This book focuses on how to strike the right balance between efficiency and flexibility. In addition, this book will show you how to close the gap between what companies need to be efficient (e.g., productivity, innovation, and results) and what employees seek (e.g., a sense of wellness and purpose) while attracting and retaining a workforce (people).

I believe the solutions lie in four themes, which, coincidentally, are also the part titles of this book.

1. **Disrupt:** Embrace and drive change. I'll show how disruption can be a catalyst for innovation and growth.
2. **Thrive:** Create a workplace where innovation and well-being go hand in hand, a place where everyone prospers.
3. **Evolve:** Ramp up learning and development of new skills. It's important for both individuals and companies to stay ahead in a fast-evolving world.
4. **Connect:** Forge real, lasting relationships, even in an automated age. Remember, human connection is irreplaceable.

Join me in uncovering what goes into the "secret sauce," and design and shape the workforce you want for tomorrow today.

Part I

DISRUPT

Innovate and adapt
Foster tech-savvy agility
Expand skill horizons

CHAPTER 1

Pioneers, Trailblazers, and Communicators

———

ON A SNOWY NEW ENGLAND DAY, I FOUND MYSELF AT Harvard for a lecture by Clayton Christensen, my guru of disruptive innovation. The session promised sharp insights into organizational resilience amid upheaval. Christensen illustrated the power of adaptive strategies in a volatile business world, highlighting examples of both triumphs and pitfalls in the face of rapid change. Those ninety minutes zipped by.

He clarified a common misconception: disruptive innovation isn't about breakthrough technologies that enhance existing services, but rather, it's about replacing old ways with new—like how streaming services ended video rentals, rendering Blockbuster's whole model obsolete. This also follows Christensen's theory that disruptive innovation starts by either targeting less demanding customers with simpler, cheaper solutions or creating a completely new market: "A disruptive innovation, by definition, starts from one of those two footholds . . . Entrants that prove disruptive begin by successfully targeting those overlooked segments, gaining a foothold by delivering more-suitable functionality—frequently at a lower price."[1]

In some instances, a change in societal attitudes drives new market segments. Consider the circus.

Cirque du Soleil has endeavored to disrupt the conventional circus industry, one that had become synonymous with questionable animal treatment, cliché clown performances, and even a "freak show." These elements had all lost their appeal over time because of shifting societal attitudes. The company's idea wasn't to change the circus but to create a new way of presenting this type of entertainment that people would not find questionable or offensive.

Cirque du Soleil truly revolutionized the circus model. They homed in on acrobatics, with human performers in stunning costumes performing their seemingly death-defying acts, and intricate, immersive set pieces. This transformation wasn't simply a change; it disrupted and transformed how people perceive and engage the whole idea of a large circus-style, spectacle form of entertainment.

Christensen's insights and Cirque du Soleil's pioneering spirit weren't just eye-openers; they fundamentally shifted my understanding of disruption. They epitomize the essence of pioneers, trailblazers, and communicators in the modern world. This was a call for me to rethink, reimagine, and reframe how we prepare people for the modern workplace. This preparation must extend beyond the conventional and embrace the unexplored and innovative.

In the sections that follow, we'll dive into the entrepreneurial spirit, the magic of creation, and unleashing trailblazer energy. Each segment ties back to our central theme: pioneering approaches in various fields, from the culinary arts to technology and business. We'll explore strategies for fostering a culture of innovation and entrepreneurship, drawing parallels between diverse realms such as the quiet vineyards of Napa Valley and the high-pressure, often chaotic world of top chefs like Marco Pierre White and Gordon Ramsay. Their stories demonstrate how embracing challenges and thinking creatively can lead to transformative success.

Ignite entrepreneurial spirit

It's time to ignite that entrepreneurial spirit within your company. We're talking innovation, risk-taking, and pushing boundaries. If you want to stay ahead of the game, you'll need to inspire your employees to pursue new ideas and unleash that creative energy that can take your company to the next level. As a manager or leader or entrepreneur, you have the power to transform your team and company. This journey starts with YOU.

By leveraging your own unique skill set and personal brand of leadership, you can create an atmosphere ripe with creativity and innovation that will lay the foundations for success. As a former chef, I suggest that you think of being a manager like being a master chef. You shouldn't be shy with your seasoning, adding a pinch of creativity here and a dash of innovation there to inject some energy and enthusiasm into your employees.

The magic of creation

There's something magical about the idea of creation, whether it's a meal, a system, or a product, such as toy cars. As a young child, I was transported into a world of wonder while reading the history of a Matchbox model car factory by Miroslav Šašek. His vivid descriptions of skilled workers crafting miniature masterpieces, armed with only drawings and photos, ignited a spark in me. Imagining the precision-packed production line, complete with six tons of molten zinc and computer-controlled die-casting machines cranking out 20 million parts each week, left me in awe. Fueled by my newly discovered passion for understanding how things were made, I began crafting my own unique creations from LEGO bricks, building practical and intricate models of factories, cars, and entire villages. To this day, Šašek's story serves as a reminder to me of the endless possibilities of creation, the thrill of discovering the unknown, and the joy of working with my head and my hands.

That book, gifted to me by my Czech grandparents, remains in my office today. The inscription reads, "To Nicky Boy, *The Good Pie Cook*, 2nd September 1972, Babi & Deda." When my gaze falls upon it, I'm reminded of my youthful wonder and aspirations.

Making a Difference

A thought—you can show someone you care and are invested in their growth, success, ambition, or dreams through a thoughtful gesture, like the gift of an inspiring book. A heartfelt message, along with some personal words of support or motivation, is a wonderful way to spark confidence.

Unleashing trailblazer energy

Trailblazers embody the innovative, independent qualities of an entrepreneur. They have no fear of taking risks. They challenge established norms in pursuit of new and innovative ideas. They are the ones who can unearth new opportunities, drive positive change, infuse growth, and make a difference in a company or even an entire industry.

But how do you find and foster these trailblazers in your workplace? It all starts with identifying the key traits and characteristics of trailblazers, and creating an environment that is highly supportive of their unique talents and abilities. Some key traits of these trailblazers include curiosity, a drive toward discovery, and excelling in joint innovation and teamwork. They are action oriented, fueled by an intrinsic motivation to succeed. They are driven by their passion for turning ideas into tangible outcomes. They are also flexible, seamlessly adapting to evolving situations. And finally, where someone else would walk away from a challenge, they see obstacles as opportunities to pivot, transition, or overcome. Trailblazers see an old abandoned lighthouse as a future mansion, last night's leftovers as the starters for today's feast, or a struggling company as a future star that will land on the front page (or home page) of the top business magazines. This is how trailblazers see the world. Look for people with this kind of vision in your company.

A wonderful story about bringing fresh ideas to life in true trailblazer fashion comes from a boutique vineyard in the town of Calistoga, in California's Napa Valley. The owners were struggling with traditional sales methods and the costs of representation in what had become a crowded market. Amidst these struggles, the winemaker thought that by identifying a few trailblazers within their team and empowering people from all parts of the operation to contribute innovative ideas, they might find a winning way to increase sales. They found several.

For example, one game changer was to reimagine traditional wine tastings, which had remained the same for decades, probably centuries. With the rise and popularity of video conferencing technology, they introduced online wine tastings that allow people from all over the world to participate remotely. This dramatically expanded the reach of the winery. Customers can now have sample kits sent to them so they can join online tastings from the comfort of their own homes, eliminating the need for travel and accommodation arrangements. As it turns out, this convenience is appealing to many consumers. It's a perfect blend of old and new thinking. Their online wine tastings are by far their most popular tasting now, though they still offer the traditional cellar-door experience for those seeking the ambiance of an in-person visit.

Finding and managing a new trailblazer mean being open to new ideas and forgetting the phrase "that's how we've always done it." Who knows? You may have a trailblazer or two already in your employ. Don't overlook their ideas. Consider the infamous story of Kodak. Back in 1975, a Kodak engineer named Steve Sasson invented the first-ever digital camera. Sasson was a trailblazer; unfortunately, Kodak did not embrace such thinking. Rather than run with the revolutionary idea, they turned it down. Not long after, other companies made a splash with digital cameras, leaving Kodak in the dust. It's the epitome of business failure stories and has reminded entrepreneurs and managers for years to be on the lookout for a trailblazer—and if you find one, don't turn them away.

Meeting a real trailblazer

Meet John "Wik" Wikstrom, a serial entrepreneur who, in 1995, cofounded an international technology company called Magic Memories. The company and its founder are driven by the passion to innovate and create hyper-personal experiences that bring customers and brands together. Decades later, Wik still radiates the entrepreneurial spirit that kick-started his success and inspires his team to strive for greatness.

Before Wik and I formed a professional connection, we first became acquainted as part of the community at PS 166 Richard Rodgers School of the Arts and Technology, in Manhattan, where my children attended elementary school. I overheard a familiar accent in the halls one day—that of John Wik. As an Aussie, I recognized the Kiwi (New Zealand) twang right away. I struck up a conversation, and our talk quickly moved past our nations' sports rivalry and shared history. This has led to a great friendship, and Wik is a wealth of inspiration for me. The following are some of the wise principles he's shared.

Five key tenets to creating trailblazer energy as a culture:

1. Set a vision that becomes so clear, it creates a purpose for all those in the organization.

2. Have a purpose that illustrates integrity. It needs to be authentic, and you need to actually be delivering on it.

3. Create a compelling narrative that sits alongside that purpose. A great narrative and an upstanding purpose create a following.

4. Continue to build a following, and ensure there is a high level of engagement. Offer consistent communication and updates on progress (both good and bad) aligned to the purpose so the narrative becomes addictive across both your organization and your customers.

5. As a leader, listen. Recognizing feedback is critical to foster a sense of belief and belonging to your mission.

Three pillars that empower a culture of innovation and performance:

1. Believing
2. Belonging
3. Contributing

Wik explained further, "When an individual feels a genuine attachment to these three pillars in an organization, you have successfully created a culture that each person is proud to be part of. The individuals hold themselves and others accountable. Pride in what you do and why you are doing it not only generates next-level performance, it also significantly increases retention of key resources, both human and capital."[2]

I like the fact that Wik, early in his business years, created a simple purpose statement: WE MAKE PEOPLE SMILE.

"We knew our products celebrated togetherness—special times, at special brands, with people we love," says Wik, adding that "we knew if we did this right, we could actually improve people's day, weeks, and, in some cases, their lives by creating and capturing magical moments that truly made people smile . . . in their bones. We determined that a smile needs no explanation [and no] translation and works for any location or demographic."[3]

What Wik was offering was genuine and authentic. Many members of his Magic Memories office consistently told him they were proud to be part of such a special team. They believed in their purpose as part of their culture.

Mastering communications

Communication is one of the most important skills in the business world, and there are many leaders who excel at it. But there's one person who stands out in my mind as a true master of communication: Marc Benioff, the CEO of Salesforce. His early years were marked by entrepreneurial spirit, founding Liberty Software as a teenager and developing games for the Atari 8. Marc's ability to communicate his vision with enthusiasm, passion, and clarity has been instrumental in turning Salesforce into a multibillion-dollar business. Marc started Salesforce in a San Francisco apartment in 1999 with a vision for the web-based software, and he ended up revolutionizing the customer relationship management industry.

Marc also has made a commitment to innovation in the workforce. We've had some great exchanges about my mission to boost apprentice-ships in the United States, aiming for the ambitious goal of 5 million sign-ons. I have to say that I am genuinely impressed with him and his efforts to advance this cause. In one conversation, I expressed my grati-tude for his bringing that 5 million target to the attention of the White House! Then, I suggested a somewhat out-of-the-box idea: what if we had an "apprenticeship czar"? (Okay, maybe it was a bit far-fetched.) The idea was to have a prominent businessperson who could effec-tively organize employers. Marc, being the down-to-earth person he is, didn't immediately jump on board; instead, he responded by saying that although he wasn't directly involved in expansion operations, he did have a wealth of ideas. One of them involved using his networks to spread the word.

So he took one of the articles I wrote for *Forbes* magazine about expanding apprenticeships and shared it within government circles and with the senior advisor to the president. That act of kindness caught me off guard; it was really thoughtful of him. The article ended up gaining traction on its own with people sharing it, leaving comments, and genu-inely getting excited about the possibility of expanding apprenticeships.

During another conversation with Marc, I mentioned how apprenticeships could truly transform millions of lives by providing both employment opportunities and economic stability—something I wholeheartedly believe in.

Marc's focus on apprenticeships and workforce development is just one example of his commitments to improving business communication and collaboration. But Marc's impact on the world extends far beyond his business success. He's also a vocal advocate for social justice and equality, and he's committed to using his platform to make a positive impact on the world. Whether he's speaking out about climate change or supporting marginalized communities, Marc is a true leader who is willing to take a stand.

Staying focused

In an HBO documentary titled *Becoming Warren Buffett*, the renowned investor recalls a conversation he had with Microsoft cofounder Bill Gates. They were asked to write down one word that helped them the most, and without conferring, Buffett and Gates each wrote down the word *focus*.

Focus is something I think about often. Where do you want to focus your time and energy? Take a moment now to pause and think about what it means to focus. Buffett describes his focus as a natural inclination to immerse himself in whatever subject interests him. He will read about it, talk about it, and make efforts to meet people involved in it. He spends a lot of time thinking about business and investment problems, and he finds it enjoyable to ponder situations and come up with solutions. However, he admits that human problems can be the most challenging.

But what does Buffett's focus look like in practice? His daughter, Susan, describes her father's intense focus, saying, "He was there physically, but he was upstairs reading all the time. I always told my mother we have to talk in sound bites. If you start going into some long thing, unless you have explained that to him ahead of time, you'll lose him to whatever giant thought he has going in his head at the time that he was probably thinking about before you came in and he really wants to get back to it."[4]

Although it may be difficult to focus to the extent Buffett does, we can all learn from his approach. It's about immersing yourself in what you're interested in and giving it your full attention.

Taking a cue from Buffett, I wanted to discover a technique I could use for improving focus. So I connected with fellow Californian Jacob Dominicus, an executive coach who teaches meditation and concentration. We discussed the importance of psychologist Mihaly Csikszentmihalyi's concept of "flow," which is a mental state of complete immersion and focus on an activity. In this state, individuals are fully engaged and absorbed in what they are doing, often experiencing a sense of timelessness and intense enjoyment. I took some classes with Jacob and learned techniques such as maintaining posture, directing and intensifying attention, and practicing metacognition (thinking about how you think). I have incorporated many of Jacob's teachings, and it has made a difference in both my business and home life.

Effective communication and interpersonal skills for leaders and managers:

- Allow employees to navigate different communication styles with adaptability, flexibility, and optimism.

- Enable employees to express themselves clearly and effectively, both verbally and nonverbally.

- Help employees understand the social and cultural context in which they are communicating.

- Allow various departments or segments of a business to learn from each other and work together as a team more efficiently.

Adaptability, flexibility, and optimism:

- Allow employees to reshape, transition, and transform themselves in their workplace in tandem with the pace of change in the marketplace.

- Help employees create a team that can work together effectively, with a common purpose, to achieve that magical connection that leads to innovation and success.

Chefpreneurs

The significance of teamwork is important, especially in a diverse global workforce. But teamwork doesn't mean everyone on the team does the same job. It is about letting people do what they do best for the benefit of the team. I learned this back when I worked at a five-star hotel in London.

After finishing my hotel studies at the prestigious École hôtelière de Lausanne, nestled in the picturesque city of Lausanne, Switzerland, I ventured back into the hustle and bustle of international kitchen life. The competition was fierce, and it was difficult to find a job in the kitchens of a prestigious hotel. However, I managed to land a position at the famous Claridge's in London, where I first met the eccentric, energetic entrepreneur Chef Mario Leznik. It was Chef Leznik who played a role in transforming Claridge's as its maître chef de cuisine. At the age of thirty-two, he embraced the challenge of revitalizing Claridge's scene with a contemporary perspective. His time at Claridge's brought about a change in the hotel's food operations, which set it on a prosperous path to become the five-star establishment it is today.

When I arrived for my first day at Claridge's, I was dispatched to the fish handling team, where I met two gentlemen from my home-land of Australia. The executive chef had assigned roles based on nationalities. The Swiss chefs were the *sauciers*, responsible for sauces. This job requires the same precision and attention to detail as watch-making, so it was no surprise that it was given to the Swiss chefs, with their historic excellence in the craft of sauce making. Meanwhile, the French chefs ran the pastry shop as *pâtissiers*, perhaps due to the French having a rich history of pastry-making. The Canadians were in charge of the cold food section, which featured a lot of smoked salmon, perhaps a nod to Canada's Northern cold. The English chefs were the *entremetiers*, responsible for vegetables, perhaps reflecting England's long-standing history of horticulture. And the Aussies were the *poissonniers*, responsible for fish dishes, presumably because of our connection to clean air and the ocean. (It's worth noting that *poisson-niers* is just a fancy French term for "fish cook," not someone skilled in poisoning people.) The funny part is that one of my fellow Aussies was from Alice Springs, which is about a thousand miles away from the nearest coastline.

The Claridge's hotel in London has a long history of interesting guests, including royalty, as well as Cary Grant, Audrey Hepburn, Katharine Hepburn, Mick Jagger, Winston Churchill, Yul Brynner, and Bing Crosby. The food was out of this world, with classic dishes like steak and kidney pie and fancy creations like salmon-en-croûte, which is essentially creamy salmon in a crusty pastry shell.

Working at Claridge's was intense, and the pressure was on to make everything perfect. We spent long hours in the kitchen, and the big bosses were constantly yelling at us to get everything right. However, I learned a lot about teamwork, camaraderie, and resilience under Chef Leznik's leadership. He was an innovator, given a budget of $15 million to renovate the kitchens, and he was all about creating the best possible space to produce the best possible food.

Looking back, I realize that my experience at Claridge's was a game changer for me. It taught me the value of hard work, perseverance, and innovation. Although Chef Leznik's approach of assigning roles based on nationalities may not be the way things are done today, I also learned the importance of respecting everyone's individuality and what they bring to the table (pun intended).

Years later, international chef and restaurateur Gordon Ramsay took over the restaurant at Claridge's and with his team received a Michelin star. As you may have seen on reality television, Gordon has his own leadership style—he is gritty and has never been afraid of a challenge. His passion, drive, and entrepreneurial spirit have made him a true force to be reckoned with on the culinary front.

I grew up and was trained in a different culinary era. I met Anthony Bourdain a few times, and he was the real deal. By that, I mean not full of his own self-importance. He was a no-nonsense, down-to-earth guy and very inspiring.

Somehow, I found myself in a yearlong consultancy position in Singapore many years back—a long way from my culinary roots. I now have a long connection with Singapore: my wife, Prue, was born and schooled there, and I have an abiding love for the city and its food. As soon as I moved there, I immersed myself in the city's unique blend of cultures and awesome flavors. One night, after a particularly draining day, I flopped down on my hotel bed without plugging in my phone, and it died during the night. The next morning, I woke to a series of messages from a great culinary mate, saying, "Hey, I'm here with Anthony Bourdain. They're gonna shoot a scene talking about Singapore's culinary world at Marina Bay Sands. We've got a seat at the table. Come down; you can be part of the show!" My heart sank. That would have been my first and only television appearance on *The Layover* with Bourdain himself. I learned an important life lesson that morning: always plug in your phone.

I also encountered characters like Marco Pierre White, a British chef, restaurateur, and television personality who rose to fame as the youngest chef ever to be awarded three Michelin stars. He became well-known from his appearances on the UK versions of *Hell's Kitchen* and *MasterChef*. He summed up the pressure chefs feel at the three-star Michelin level by famously commenting about diners coming to his restaurant: "If I came to your house for dinner an hour late, then criticized all your furniture and your wife's haircut and said all your opinions were stupid, how would you feel? People still come here and expect a three-course meal in an hour. What do they think I do—pull rabbits out of a fucking hat? I'm not a magician."[5]

The point of all of these adventures is that the world of culinary art is filled with both magic and madness. It's not about pulling rabbits out of a hat but about embracing the chaos, the pressure, and sometimes the unconventional wisdom of chefs like Marco Pierre White. The vibrant mix of cultures, the intensity of expectations, and the unending quest for perfection make the kitchen a place where ordinary food transforms into extraordinary experiences. As a chefpreneur, you must navigate this chaotic beauty with grace and an understanding that every challenge is an opportunity to learn, grow, and create something truly remarkable.

The idea of embracing the "anarchy" (i.e., madness, chaos, and pressure) that takes place in a kitchen can be found in all types of businesses. Whether it's the heat of the kitchen, the chill of a failed business transaction, or the warmth of success, every aspect shapes the soul of a true entrepreneur. In the world of culinary arts, we can all learn from innovators like Leznik, Ramsay, and White. Likewise, in business, we learn from innovators such as Nikola Tesla, Steve Jobs, Sheryl Sandberg, Jeff Bezos, and Daymond John, all of whom embraced the power of creativity and individuality.

Managers, leaders, and business owners should also value these qualities. This means seeking chefs with unique backgrounds and skills, employees who have had enlightening experiences. It means looking for abilities, talents, and skills that show up both on and off the resume or menu. It also means being open and listening to the ideas, concepts, and recipes these people bring to your business.

In a hectic world, taking the time to focus on the important topics can lead to positive outcomes for both you and your company. Navigating the ever-challenging business world can be daunting, but don't let that get you down. Reflecting on your personal and professional meaning will help you find both success and happiness amidst all of life's chaos.

CHAPTER 2

Embrace Change in the Evolving Landscape

———

CHANGE IS A GIVEN IN THE BUSINESS WORLD, AND IF YOU want to stay ahead of the curve, you need to be agile and adaptable. This means embracing new technologies, processes, and business models and being open to new ways of doing things. If you have a mindset that "we've always done it that way, so why should we change?" you will inevitably fall behind. The market will continue to change whether you are a part of that change or not. It's like a train leaving the station: it will depart whether you're on it or not. Remember that although change may be frightening at first, if you take some time to research and understand how the change can be beneficial, you may see greater possibilities for success. Change can open doors to new possibilities. Study them carefully, but don't wait too long, or you'll be left standing there while the train (or the market) forges ahead.

Every change is not a winner!

Not all changes succeed, but there are businesses that refuse to budge, and as a result, they very often fail. (Just ask Blockbuster, Kodak, or Toys-"R"-Us.)

Of course, the best scenario for a business is to *be* the change that disrupts the status quo and makes a mark in the business landscape. But before you can change the landscape of business as we know it today, consider how solid, well researched, and tested the new ideas are throughout your organization. Gauge what the level of support for them could be.

Before making changes, it's best to test your idea. This will significantly minimize your risk. Have you ever tried a new recipe for the first time, only to realize that it's a complete flop? Maybe you added too much of one ingredient, left out another entirely, or forgot a crucial step. Just like a failed Thanksgiving feast, rushed innovation in any workplace can sometimes lead to costly mistakes. That's why in the kitchen, we do what's called a test bake. This entails making a small amount of food for test purposes, to get feedback without spending too much money or taking a great risk.

In the business world, the equivalent would be a prototype or proof of concept of a new idea. Teams can identify issues or concerns and make the necessary adjustments before launching it to a wider audience. This approach can help save money by preventing costly mistakes or large-scale failed projects, which can result in wasted resources, time, and money. Rather than taking a "throw everything at the wall and see what sticks" approach, prototyping an idea allows teams to experiment in a controlled setting and make any necessary adjustments.

It's the same with cooking: not every test bake will turn out perfectly the first time. But by taking the time to test out ideas on a smaller scale, teams can learn from their mistakes, refine their approach, and ultimately create a more successful final product.

So the next time your team has a new innovative idea, consider doing a test bake. Include your team and maybe even some customers to provide feedback.

Final note: if the test bake is a disaster, don't even think of giving up. Do you know how many unsuccessful test bakes a chef goes through before striking recipe gold? Many! Believe me! It is unlikely that you will discover your special sauce on your first try. Remember that when making changes, you may not land exactly where you want immediately, but failures very often lead to great success.

Combining technology and the human touch

The rise of artificial intelligence (AI) along with automation and other technologies has had a profound effect on the future of work. By eliminating mundane, low-skilled tasks, technology allows workers to focus on higher-value activities that have the power to drive global economic growth. Although this shift can bring some uncertainty into the job market, it also opens up new opportunities for workers with the right skills and qualifications.

As technology continues to evolve, you need to get a handle on ethics and privacy, from both moral and legal perspectives. We're all concerned about people getting our personal information, and rightfully so. Privacy is one aspect that should be taken into account when using any type of technology, especially when creating customer listings or personnel files. People have a right to know how their personal data are being used or shared. Moreover, when developing AI systems, there must be considerations for human bias in algorithms and training data that could result in systemic inequity or discriminatory outcomes. It is essential to prioritize a human-centered approach to technology, empowering individuals while protecting their rights and providing enriching job experiences. Understanding AI and its capabilities allows us to work alongside machines effectively, turning them into partners rather than threats. Technology can also open up exciting new opportunities, creating entirely new industries and job pathways. We must embrace the potential benefits of technology while being mindful not to allow it to detract from the importance of human judgment, creativity, intuition, empathy, and other qualities that (thus far) only humans possess.

Car manufacturer Toyota is known for its innovative approach to manufacturing and use of *autonomation*, or "automation with a human touch." This is a manufacturing approach that combines automation and human problem-solving to improve efficiency and quality control.

At the heart of Toyota's autonomation process is a sensor system that continuously monitors the factory line for any malfunctions or defects. When a problem is detected, the line is automatically stopped, and a display board alerts a human supervisor to the issue. This high-tech sensor system means that human workers don't have to monitor every line constantly, freeing them up to focus on other tasks.

Meanwhile, if a problem is identified, Toyota's autonomation system works with humans to solve it. The system analyzes the problem to determine its root cause and then separates the work into human tasks and machine tasks. This approach allows humans to focus on tasks that require problem-solving and critical thinking while machines handle more precise and repetitive tasks.

Additionally, by balancing automation with human engagement, Toyota has been able to improve efficiency, quality control, and worker satisfaction. The success of their approach is a testament to the power of combining human problem-solving with the precision of machines.

However, Toyota's autonomation system does present some challenges. Initially, the line was slower because of the frequent shutdowns. Over time, though, the system became more efficient as both humans and machines learned and continuously improved. By working together, humans and machines are able to create a more efficient and effective manufacturing process that leverages the strengths of both.

Autonomation provides a prime example of how humans and automated machines can work together to create a more efficient and effective manufacturing process. As other companies adopt similar approaches, we can expect to see even more innovation and progress in the world of manufacturing.

The dark side of technology and automation

The rise of advanced technology and artificial intelligence will cause a tectonic shift in the way we work, with an increasing number of jobs becoming obsolete because of automation. At the same time, the demand for technologies is likely to create more jobs than they displace; governments and organizations need to provide support for those displaced so that they can acquire the new skills needed in the modern workplace. As we automate more tasks, it's crucial to invest in retraining programs that equip our workforce with new skills, ensuring they remain relevant and competitive.

In the face of job loss, the fear and stress of displacement can make it feel like the walls are crashing in. The truth is that, automation has been slowly taking human jobs for quite a while. Assembly lines and machines have replaced manual labor in many industries, from agriculture and transport to manufacturing and more. Advancements in AI, robotics, and voice recognition have also steadily increased in recent years, leaving many feeling witless as they search for other options. Although technology can create new opportunities, the worry over job displacement remains a reality that workers must face, wrapped up together with an array of new business challenges.

As technology progresses, governments, businesses, education systems, and individuals *can* work together to create support systems and training programs that allow displaced workers to acquire new skills and remain competitive in the modern economy. Social safety nets and training programs are essential in ensuring that workers losing their jobs because of technology (whether it's automation or AI) are not permanently left behind in this new economic landscape.

Managers need to be aware of these risks and plan accordingly. We cannot afford to overlook the human element in the workforce as a whole, or we risk creating a society where the few benefit at the expense of the many.

Corporate reskilling programs

It's heartening to see that progress is already being made. According to the *Harvard Business Review*, "Infosys [an information technology consulting company] has reskilled more than 2,000 cybersecurity experts with various adjacent competencies and capability levels." This same article, titled "Reskilling in the Age of AI," also points out that "through its Machine Learning University, [Amazon] has enabled thousands of employees who initially had little experience in machine learning to become experts in the field."[1]

Although these changes may seem daunting, they also present an opportunity for transformation and progress. As we navigate this new economic landscape, keep in mind that the future of work may be very different from what we know today. As more jobs become automated, the demand for workers with a diverse range of skills is likely to increase. To remain competitive, workers will need to adapt to new technologies and acquire new skills to fill new demands.

Five factors necessary to move forward with the times:

- Agility
- Adaptability
- Accountability
- Flexibility
- Ongoing learning

The healthcare sector, for example, is taking advantage of the opportunities that automation and AI technologies present, from streamlining administrative processes to improving patient care. Although there were some initial hurdles to overcome, such as retraining staff and ensuring data privacy, these advancements offer many benefits—from increased efficiency in workflow to improved patient outcomes. The industry is exploring the potential advantages of integrating automated technologies into healthcare systems and how it can empower healthcare professionals while creating positive changes for patients as well.

With careful planning and preparation, we can create a future in which humans and technology can coexist seamlessly, much like we saw in the earlier Toyota example.

Navigating automation

Automation is not new—it's been around for centuries. Unlike AI and other technologies that include problem-solving tasks, analysis, or skills that rely on mathematics or scientific equations, automation involves having machines take over physical, typically repetitive tasks. From watermills and steam engines to automated flour mills and, of course, the well-documented assembly lines used by Henry Ford, automation has been with us for a long time.

What has also been around for a long time is the fear of new technologies that may replace workers at many levels in the near future. However, with growing advancements in automation over recent years, there are more valid reasons for concern than ever before.

The future of work is uncertain, but making sure your company stays informed, armed, involved, and ready with the necessary skills, abilities, individuals and businesses, you can embrace the opportunities that technology presents. By investing in education and training and embracing new technologies, we can create a future in which automation is a source of progress and not a source of fear and insecurity.

Taking on the dangerous jobs

Many dangerous jobs that once put human lives at risk are now being performed by automation. Remember the Fukushima nuclear plant leak in Japan? Robots were deployed to inspect damaged reactors and collect radioactive debris, minimizing human exposure to dangerous levels of radiation. Unmanned drones are now used for military resupply missions as well as for gathering intelligence, surveillance, reconnaissance, search and rescue missions, logistics, and training. Using drones can minimize risk for soldiers, which in turn can reduce casualties. Unfortunately, drones can also malfunction, which jeopardizes the safety of military personnel and civilians.

Technology has also been utilized in hazardous activities such as deep-sea diving, explosive ordnance disposal, and mining operations.

A crash course on the rise of technology: learning from history

What can we learn from history? Change can bring anxiety, yet every workplace innovation is an opportunity for growth. Take William Lee, for example, who, in 1590, wanted to produce stockings faster for Queen Elizabeth I, only to see his patent denied because of her fear of the impact it would have on people. "Thou aimest high, Master Lee," she told the clergyman. "Consider thou what the invention could do to my poor subjects. It would assuredly bring to them ruin by depriving them of employment, thus making them beggars."[2]

In the early 1800s, a group of skilled artisans known as the Luddites waged an ultimately unsuccessful battle against mechanization. This advancement threatened their livelihoods and caused them to sabotage textile machines to protect their hard-earned craftsmanship. However, this technological development was eventually beneficial for society: agriculturists whose jobs were altered or taken over by machines found new opportunities in less dangerous and better paying professions than they had before. Today, people who are anti-technology are still called Luddites.

In 1900, half of America's population worked on farms; today, that number has dropped to 2 percent, largely because of advances in technology that allowed would-be farmers other avenues of employment with greater benefits for themselves and their families. Although a small portion of Americans remain dedicated to farmwork, they are producing an abundance and variety of foods, easily meeting domestic demand with plenty to spare for foreign markets. This has created new jobs in packing, loading, shipping, and selling, which has greatly increased food supply to buyers worldwide.

JFK on the perils of factory automation

During the early 1960s, as automation began to threaten employment opportunities everywhere in America, President John F. Kennedy stepped up. In a historic address best remembered for inspiring our nation to aim toward putting a man on the moon, Kennedy addressed potential joblessness due to automation. Though few recall his words on the topic, his infamous challenge still rings true today:

"I am therefore transmitting to the Congress a new Manpower and Training Development program to train or retrain several hundred thousand workers, particularly in those areas where we have seen chronic unemployment as a result of technological factors in new occupational skills over a four-year period, in order to replace those skills made obsolete by automation and industrial change with the new skills which the new processes demand."[3]

Through resilience and determination, the nation overcame a looming threat of automation-induced unemployment without relying on the government's involvement. Many such initiatives still fall short today—putting us at risk for another wave of job losses in this new industrial age. As JFK warned decades ago, we must take proactive measures now to face potential worker displacement due to technological advances; these are no longer distant worries but very real possibilities that should be taken seriously.

With each passing century, the way we work changes drastically—from the days of manually tilling fields and crafting tools to our current online-centric world. To understand these seismic shifts in labor trends over time, let's explore four major revolutions that have shaped how we learn, live, and do business today.

The Last 250 Years

 1760s   **First Industrial Revolution**
Invention of the steam engine and railroads

 1870s   **The Machine Age**
Electricity, automation of factory processes, and a worldwide economy

 1960s   **The Digital Age**
Personal computers, the internet, and the advent of virtual infrastructures

 1980s   **The Personal Computing Era**
Machines gain the ability to beat human chess masters

 2010s   **The Age of Machine Learning**
Automation, robotics, big data, and artificial intelligence

The First Revolution: Iron and Steel (1760–1840) —laying the foundation for modern industry

The first revolution saw the rise of iron and steel production. This industrial revolution brought with it an unprecedented increase in production capacity and efficiency. Inventions like the steam engine, which allowed for mass production and transportation, drastically changed the way labor was organized. As a result, factories replaced craft-based workshops as businesses became larger and increasingly complex. With new technologies came new social classes, such as managers and employers who were a pay grade above regular workers in factories and mines.

The Second Revolution: Mechanization and Automation (1870–1914)—the dawn of modern industry

The second revolution saw increasing mechanization and automation of factory processes through innovations such as assembly lines and interchangeable parts. With new technologies came new forms of labor organization. Factory jobs became more specialized, with workers performing one specific task over and over rather than mastering an entire process from start to finish. These changes also introduced new roles in management, such as supervisors who monitored worker performance on the shop floor.

The Third Revolution: Automation and Digital Tech (1969–2010)—a new era of work

The third revolution was driven by digital technology such as computing power, internet access, AI, robotics, automation, machine learning, and more. With this new wave of technology came a shift away from traditional labor organization models toward more flexible working arrangements. Companies began relying less on physical infrastructure such as offices or factories, instead opting for virtual infrastructures that enabled them to scale quickly without needing large amounts of capital expenditure upfront. Additionally, AI-enabled tools were used to reinvent processes such as customer service and sales operations.

The Fourth Industrial Revolution: AI, Robotics, VR, and IoT (2010–Present)— embracing the future of work

We're entering a world of remarkable, futuristic advancement that marks the beginning of the Fourth Industrial Revolution. It's an age when AI and robotics are inextricably intertwined with our daily lives, playing a major part in how we communicate, interact, and do business. And let's not forget virtual reality (VR), which has created an entirely new sphere of possibilities. Immersive virtual experiences are no longer something out of science-fiction novels or blockbuster movies but a reality. Coupled with the rising ubiquity of the Internet of Things (IoT), which refers to physical objects with embedded sensors, software, and other technologies for the purpose of connecting and exchanging information between devices, we're on the cusp of creating a new kind of connectedness that will redefine life as we know it.

The Fifth Industrial Revolution and Beyond—imagining the future of work

As we gaze toward the horizon of the unknown, it's easy to feel adrift in a sea of uncertainty. What exactly will the Fifth Industrial Revolution bring? Will it be a time of unimaginable innovation and prosperity, or will we be forced to confront an era of upheaval and chaos? One thing is certain: the future is full of magic and wonder, just waiting to be discovered. History shows us that with each industrial revolution, although some jobs were lost, many more were created, requiring new skills and ways of thinking.

Let's take a moment to think about video calling technology as it was first introduced in the 1960s television series *Star Trek*. When the series first aired, video conferencing was nothing more than a dream. Yet my father watched in amazement as Captain Kirk communicated face-to-face over great distances, sometimes with those inhabiting other planets, using this futuristic technology.

Fast forward to today: although Klingon as a language has not yet caught on, video conferencing and video chat technology is a popular reality. Using video conferencing at home, at work, for medical appointments, and more has become ingrained into our culture. It all comes down to, "Beam me up, Scotty!" It's almost as if the writers and creators of *Star Trek* were giving us a glimpse into the future all those years ago. What will be the next piece of science fiction to become a reality? And more importantly, how will it change the way we live and work?

CHAPTER 3

Shaping Tomorrow's Workforce Today

———

WANT A TALENTED AND DIVERSE WORKFORCE? KEEN TO attract and retain top talent? Then you need to create a workplace culture that values employee well-being and personal growth. This means creating an inclusive and supportive environment that fosters collaboration, innovation, and creativity.

My unlikely story of transitioning from the culinary world as a chef to joining the corporate world led me on an interesting journey. I soon realized that I had some control over my success and that investing in me paid off. Of course, in any work environment, luck and timing are also factors.

Steven Bradbury, the unlikely hero of the 2002 Winter Olympics in Salt Lake City, serves as an example. The talented young speed skater had a dream of winning Australia's first-ever gold medal in the Winter Games. In the final race, the competition was fierce, with the top skaters racing neck in neck down on the ice. But suddenly, disaster struck, and one by one, the other skaters crashed into one another and fell like dominos. It was a heart-stopping moment, but Bradbury was somehow able to remain standing and glided effortlessly to the finish line, securing Australia's first-ever Winter Olympics gold medal. It was a stunning victory, a truly unforgettable moment. Sometimes it takes capitalizing on an unexpected event or having a bit of luck that opens opportunities to succeed.

My corporate career started with a Bradbury-style moment. With an unexpected turn of events and the abrupt departure of my manager, I was suddenly thrust into the role of general manager in corporate HR. In my time at the company, I worked under four different CEOs and nine different managers. I got to see many different leadership styles in action on the front line. Taking my own advice, I tried to learn as much as I could from this revolving door of managers and the CEOs. Remember, lifelong learning is so important.

Learning and luck often go hand in hand. I was lucky to have gained the position in the first place, but I remained in it because I continued learning at my job. Conversely, Bradbury's training and hard work got him to the Olympics. He then had timing and good fortune on his side to win a gold medal. Learning/training and a bit of good luck make up many success stories.

Attract, retain, develop

It's often said you hire people for what they know—their technical skills—but you end up firing them for who they are. More often than not, it's because they lack certain attributes or people skills.

Regardless of whether you're attracting new talent, looking to retain current employees, or developing your staff, understanding these three themes is crucial. As we navigate through this book, we'll discuss their impact in various contexts.

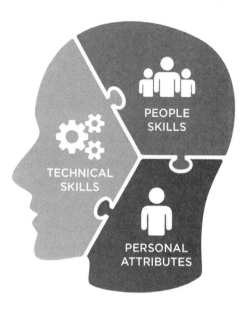

- **Technical skills:** These are specific, measurable abilities acquired through training, education, and practice, essential for executing job-specific tasks effectively. They are the foundational skills required for specific jobs, essentials that qualified candidates must have. However, because of technological advancements, these skills are constantly changing. Technical skills can be easily quantified. Trained technicians, engineers, lawyers, and doctors have certifications from training institutions. Both employers and employees must actively invest in keeping their technical skills updated.

- **People skills:** These often fall under the term "soft skills" and are actually behavioral and interpersonal skills. They relate to how effectively people interact with others and handle different workplace situations. These are often the skills that will help someone get, and keep, the job. Key skills here include communication and teamwork—the essentials for effective collaboration and networking. They are fundamental for enhancing team dynamics and are crucial in both attracting the right talent and retaining productive teams. People skills can be learned (as long as people are open-minded).

- **Personal attributes:** Although these personal characteristics can be developed, they are most often innate. For example, creative people have an ability to approach problems and situations with innovative thinking and original solutions. This is one of the things I look for, particularly in young people, along with curiosity and a strong desire to learn, understand, and explore. And, of course, another important personal attribute is resilience: the capacity to recover quickly from difficulties and adapt to adversity or change. For example, say you realize that the technical skills you learned last month may now be outdated. It takes resilience to accept that and move on. You can develop attributes, but it's akin to muscle building: it requires consistent effort and a conducive environment to truly strengthen these qualities.

Bottom line for employers: attract talent with strong technical skills, retain them through fostering soft people skills, and develop their potential by nurturing key personal attributes like adaptability and resilience. It's a three-pronged approach—hire for what they can do, keep them for how they gel with the team, and invest in their growth by enhancing their innate strengths. This is a winning formula for a team that is technically proficient, great at collaboration, and can pivot with ease to meet change.

Traits you want to see in your employees

To truly thrive, your business needs employees who

- Are honest
- Are trustworthy
- Possess strong work ethics
- Have integrity
- Demonstrate emotional intelligence and decision-making skills.

You've probably heard the phrase "slow to hire, quick to fire." Although I understand this way of thinking, I don't believe it's an optimal strategy. I believe in hiring with caution and carefully assessing a candidate's technical skills along with their personal traits and attributes in hopes of avoiding the need for termination.

Understanding the art of talent evaluation

Hiring is more art than science, a balancing act that requires a keen sense of what makes a candidate tick beyond the resume. In my journey through the corporate world, I've seen my share of hiring processes, from the overly elaborate to the disarmingly simple. The key takeaway? It's not the complexity of the process but the depth of understanding of the candidate. A resume might list achievements and skills, but it's the face-to-face, or even virtual, interactions that reveal the true measure of a potential team member.

Creating the right environment to see how candidates interact with your teams is also crucial. Although some may prefer the formality of an office setting for interviews, I've found that a relaxed atmosphere can lead to more genuine exchanges. The goal is to peel back the layers and get a glimpse of the person behind the professional façade. It's about seeing how they mesh with the existing team and the culture you've nurtured rather than just slotting a skill set into an open position.

This approach extends to every stage of the interview process, from casual meet-ups to more structured interactions within the workplace. It's about observation and engagement, gauging how a candidate navigates different scenarios and interacts with potential future colleagues. A more detailed blueprint on executing these strategies effectively awaits you in Chapter 13.

And yes, the due diligence of reference checks cannot be overstated—real conversations offer insights into a candidate's work ethic, dedication, and how they've contributed to communities or teams in the past. It's about discerning commitment, not just competence.

Encountering candidates that leave you on the fence is also part of the process. Here, patience is essential. Giving them space to reflect and reach out shows their level of interest and, importantly, their initiative. It's a telling sign of their desire to be part of the team.

Firing: it's a dirty job, but someone has to do it—and do it right

Firing someone is never easy, but with proper planning and preparation, it can be a manageable task. In my experience, I've learned a few valuable lessons that I want to share with you. First and foremost, documentation is essential. It's important to have a paper trail to protect yourself legally and to ensure you're making decisions that are in the best interest of the company.

When it comes time to have the conversation, remember that less is more. This is not a debate or negotiation; the decision has already been made. Before taking any action, it's wise to consider and seek professional input on tricky situations that may arise. An outside perspective can offer valuable advice and help you navigate any potential challenges. During the termination itself, it's crucial to use the past tense. This avoids any misunderstandings or arguments that could derail the conversation.

And finally, I have a cautionary tale to share about an operations manager whom we'll call Anne (not her real name). Anne once handled a termination rather badly. She arrived at the office of the employee she was about to fire, only to be greeted with warmth and hospitality. Instead of getting straight to the point, Anne engaged in casual conversation about the weather and even accepted a cup of tea from the employee. It was during this friendly chat over tea that she finally revealed the purpose of her visit. Needless to say, it didn't end well.

Learn from Anne's mistake and always approach terminations professionally, directly, and respectfully.

What do other managers and leaders think?

Curious about what people in hiring positions value most? Here are the most common responses from my straw poll:

- **Adaptability and problem-solving:** Employers need employees who can adapt to new strategies, environments, and changes and are creative in finding solutions to challenges.

- **Resilience and proactivity:** Companies value employees who can handle stress and challenges, return stronger, and initiate on improvement and growth.

- **Cooperation and flexibility:** Teamwork is critical, and employers seek candidates who are team players and can quickly adapt to new situations and shifting priorities.

Let's talk fusion: from kitchens to boardrooms

As someone who loves Asian fusion as a food style, I've always been fascinated by the creativity and innovation that goes into combining different flavors, ingredients, and cooking techniques to create something entirely new and unique. Take for example XO sauce, a spicy seafood sauce that epitomizes Asian fusion cuisine. Originating in Hong Kong during the 1980s, XO sauce blends ingredients from Cantonese and Western cooking, combining dried seafood like scallops and shrimp with garlic, prosciutto, fish sauce, ginger, chili peppers, and shallots. The name "XO" comes from the term "extra old," used to describe high-quality aged cognac. Still today, XO sauce is used as a condiment or as seasoning in a variety of dishes, including stir-fries, seafood dishes, and noodles.

Let's take the same spirit of fusion and innovation behind XO sauce and use it to think about skills in the workplace. Just as combining diverse culinary elements can create unique and flavorful dishes, merging different skills, backgrounds, and personalities in an organization can lead to innovative solutions and a dynamic workplace. This approach, akin to a chef experimenting with various ingredients to achieve the perfect balance of flavors, involves identifying and blending the distinct abilities and experiences of employees to enhance creativity, productivity, and collaboration. By fostering an environment where diverse skills are valued and leveraged in novel ways, organizations can unlock new possibilities and drive success, much like the delicious and inventive creations in Asian fusion cuisine. (And about that XO sauce recipe, Michelle Tam and Henry Fong have it just right in their *Nom Nom Paleo* book series.)

How to unleash a fusion approach in your workforce

First, you'll want to conduct a skills audit to identify critical gaps and opportunities for talent optimization. Analyze the skills and capabilities of your existing workforce to identify individuals with complementary skill sets, backgrounds, and personalities who may work well together. For example, in a software development firm, a skills assessment unveiled an engineer's passion for graphic design, resulting in their active involvement in UI/UX (user interface/user experience) tasks, which greatly enhanced the overall aesthetics of the product.

Create a plan for retraining and redeploying existing talent rather than hiring new full-time employees. Identify critical gaps in your organization's talent resources, and create a plan to address evolving business needs based on your company's future plans and goals. For example, one retail chain successfully implemented a program that improved the literacy of its store managers, enabling them to manage online sales channels. Upskilling and reskilling initiatives like this one can lead to success by maximizing the potential of your current workforce while positioning your company for expansion in the digital era. By investing in the skills of your current employees, you can confidently navigate sales channels with future plans for digital expansion and achieve revenue growth. This approach is not only cost effective but forward thinking, ensuring that your company remains competitive and prosperous.

Try team fusion

You can build team fusion by pairing unlikely employees on projects—
people from different departments from different generations, with
varying skill sets and/or diverse backgrounds. By creating such diverse
teams and encouraging cross-functional collaboration, you open your
company to being more innovative, inspired by unexpected solutions.

Fusion also means breaking down silos and promoting the
exchange of ideas to forge more effective and innovative solutions.
During the COVID-19 pandemic, for example, Henry Ford Health
System in Detroit exemplified cross-functional collaboration in their
response to the unprecedented healthcare crisis. Physician anesthesi-
ologists, traditionally operating in surgical environments, pivoted to
serve in critical care units and ICUs. Their expertise in intubation,
ventilation strategies, and critical care medicine became instrumental in treating patients with severe respiratory complications
caused by the virus. Gary Loyd, M.D., a physician anesthesiologist
and director of perioperative surgery at Henry Ford Health System,
said, "Everybody felt like they were part of the solution and worked
harder. I worked a lot of night shifts and at 10 p.m., I was still seeing communications coming from administrators."[1] No one could
have anticipated a worldwide pandemic as one of the challenges
modern-day organizations would face, but the changes and new
exigencies brought by the pandemic demonstrate just how crucial
cross-functional collaboration can be in unprecedented times.

A culture of inventors and innovation

We touched upon inventors and innovators earlier when we discussed
trailblazers. Often inventors and innovators are trailblazers, but trail-

blazers may also be those who present new visions and ideas but need innovators to make them come to life.

One way to stay in front of your competitors is to invent and innovate new solutions to improve your business, your industry, and/ or the lives of your customers. But before you can foster a culture of innovation, you must first distinguish invention from innovation. An invention involves creating a completely new product or service from scratch. For instance, the Wright brothers invented the airplane. In 1903, after four years of research and development, they created the first successful powered airplane, the Wright Flyer. It was a totally new manner of transportation not built on someone else's original creation. Inventors like the Wright brothers conceive groundbreaking ideas and bring them to life. In contrast, innovation entails examining existing products, systems, or modes of transportation or communications and finding new ways to enhance them; the Apple iPod is one example, an innovation on the handheld music players of the past.

Let's delve into some proven strategies and examples of how inventors and innovators have successfully turned their ideas into profitable ventures.

Being an inventor goes beyond technical expertise and innovative thinking. It requires perseverance and determination to turn ideas into viable products or services. The journey of invention is filled with challenges like financial obstacles, marketplace resistance, and skepticism from peers and experts. Inventors push the boundaries of what we know by solving complex problems and introducing technologies once thought impossible but that we now often take for granted. They play a crucial role in driving progress and shaping our world. As such, inventors also carry responsibilities. Their creations can have profound impacts on people's lives, which means keeping ethical use in mind when considering potential consequences. Although many inventions receive recognition for their positive contributions, we should acknowledge the potential downsides as well.

Innovators

As for innovators, the list is long. Bill Gates revolutionized computers, Steve Jobs transformed cell phones, and Elon Musk transformed electric cars without inventing them. They are innovators who significantly redesigned previous inventions into far more advanced, mass-market products to meet many more customer needs than originally planned. It is such innovation that can cause disruptions in an industry. Innovation doesn't stop with products. As we have seen, we have changed the way we use a phone, from the one hanging on the kitchen wall to the one we carry with us every day. Consider the innovations in shipping, from boats, trains, and airlines to a combination of all of the above. It used to take months to deliver a letter anywhere, but now, using various modes of transportation, Amazon can get you the product you ordered almost before you know it. Even credit cards have changed significantly: some of us are old enough to remember handing the card to a cashier who had to call someone to approve the purchase. Now you tap the credit card against an enabled payment terminal to complete the transaction in seconds.

Let's also consider innovations in personal transportation. Take, for instance, electric scooters, or e-scooters, which have surged in popularity throughout Europe in recent years thanks to their sustainability and convenience, particularly for urban commutes. Although this mode of transport provides easier city navigation, many cities are facing challenges regarding safety concerns and sidewalk congestion.

Consequently, some cities have implemented restrictions or even outright bans on these modes of transport in certain areas. Nonetheless, e-scooters have become a $33 billion business worldwide.

Another new innovative means of transportation was introduced in 2001, when Segways hit the market. These two-wheeled, self-balancing devices share many qualities with e-scooters, but they did not catch on because they did not offer value innovation. They were costly, needed frequent charging, moved slowly, and were often too large and heavy to carry into a building, let alone load into a vehicle. As a result, I see Segways as more of a novelty rather than a common mode of transport that achieved widespread adoption. Nonetheless, these personal vehicles exemplify the spirit of innovation and the willingness to explore new possibilities.

Innovation also happens in the realm of processes and systems. In education, for instance, new teaching methods and tools are constantly being developed to enhance learning outcomes. The advent of VR and augmented reality offers exciting opportunities for interactive and immersive learning experiences. Even in daily activities such as shopping, we have seen great innovations in recent decades. For example, pricing on items has evolved from price stickers requiring a cashier to key in the price to electronic coding and scanning that allows a computer to bring up the price automatically.

Innovators also face challenges, which include:

- Securing funding for new ideas
- Encountering resistance to change
- Overcoming the fear of failure when it comes to risk-taking
- Proving ownership of an idea and securing it with trademarks or patents

With the right mindset and strategies in place, you can nurture your ability to think innovatively. So how can you cultivate your innovative thinking skills? It all starts with curiosity. Embrace an open-minded approach by asking questions and exploring various possibilities. Avoid confining yourself to conventional modes of thinking; instead, welcome creativity and venture beyond established boundaries. By actively seeking out fresh perspectives and ideas, collaborating with diverse individuals, and embracing the lessons learned from failure, you can jump-start your journey as an innovator.

Many innovations come from someone simply saying, "I wish there was an easier/better/cheaper way to . . ." For instance, there must be an easier way to navigate a route than trying to look at a map while you're driving. Here comes the innovative thinking: what if we had technology that could let us know the route ahead and even tell us how to get somewhere so we could drive more attentively with both hands on the steering wheel? Voilà! The GPS. It's all about having an idea to solve a common problem or make something easier or more cost effective. For example, once upon a time, someone must have asked, *why can't I watch classic movies like* Casablanca *or* The Godfather *at home whenever I feel like it?* Thanks to innovative thinking, these films and many others came into your home via VHS tapes, and now you can stream them on demand. Yes, you can have innovations upon innovations.

How to build a skilled and effective workforce for your business

Building a supportive and collaborative environment is so important for fostering creativity and productivity. However, there is no one-size-fits-all formula for building a skilled and effective workforce.

First, before building a team, have a goal in mind. Then factor in all of the activities your team or teams need to accomplish to benefit the company. Do you need people in sales? Finance? Marketing? IT? Designers? Coders? Perhaps a chef? What positions should be filled on your team, and how will members work together to achieve the goals of the business? Look for people who are autonomous workers, good decision-makers, flexible, and open to experimentation and exploration. The goals should energize your team for success.

Another important factor to consider when building a strong workforce is hiring for fit and compatibility with the team rather than just on the basis of individual qualifications. This involves looking beyond technical skills to consider how potential employees align with your company's values and culture. To create the future you want to see, you might adopt an all-around skills-based approach to hiring and development, which can lead to a more adaptable and resilient workforce.

On a particularly rainy day in Louisville, Kentucky, I attended a Grow with Google live training event. This greater initiative helps equip people with tools and knowledge to navigate the digital landscape, be it for career advancement, kick-starting small to midsize business growth, or simply broadening their skill sets. Grow with Google serves as a bridge across the digital divide, offering an array of free training courses in person and online that touch on everything from data analytics to UX design, and the recently introduced career certificates include cybersecurity and advanced fields like business intelligence and data analytics.

The event was bustling with more than seven hundred attendees, undeterred by the torrential downpour. Some folks I met were there to polish up their skills; one attendee told me she was there to upskill for a new job, hopefully in IT support. The event had a buzz. One young man I spoke with told me he was a startup entrepreneur hoping to discover "emerging digital strategies." Good for him. (I think he was there also hoping to snag some cool merch. I would have been happy with a Google promo umbrella, unfortunately, I found no such thing that day.) Events like this show people how they can use skills to advance their careers or business interests.

Onboarding

Making a good first impression counts, especially when a new employee is joining a business. Proper onboarding can set the tone for what could be a twenty-five-year career or, if done very poorly, could lead to an employee leaving before lunch.

Let's start out with some numbers. Hey, don't worry—this isn't going to turn into some stuffy academic journal filled with endless references and mind-numbing facts and figures about employee retention. But there are a couple of statistics that are definitely worth paying attention to. According to a 2022 article from the National Society of Leadership and Success (NSLS), 51 percent of Gen Z employees (individuals born between 1997 and 2009) say that their education has not prepared them to enter the workforce. In addition, a report by Deloitte estimates that the Gen Z labor force will reach 30 million by 2025, making up approximately 14 percent of the total US workforce.

Young adults starting their first jobs in the past few years have had to navigate a new professional environment shaped by the COVID-19 pandemic. Many of these young workers started their jobs remotely, without the benefit of in-person orientation or integration into their new company culture. As a result, some may not have received the same level of training, support, and feedback that they would have received if they had started their jobs with an in-person onboarding process.

According to the NSLS article, the pandemic disrupted traditional education and limited opportunities to observe professional norms and behaviors within organizations, which made it more difficult for young adults to understand what is appropriate or effective in their respective companies.

While the peak of the pandemic is behind us, employers can still support young adults starting their careers by creating intentional connections among employees across geographic and generational boundaries. This includes enabling employee choice and autonomy, setting a clear structure and purpose for interactions, and even incorporating a sense of humor and fun.

For example, employers can ask employees to complete a connection preference assessment that lets their managers know exactly how they want to engage with coworkers. Structuring interactions around clear norms and organizational values, such as specifying which meetings require participants to be on video and which do not, removes confusion and doubt, making it easier for employees to participate more freely. Letting teams codefine norms for interactions and communication can make employees feel more comfortable.

Effective onboarding is a key strategy in the "attract, retain, develop" model, ensuring that newcomers assimilate smoothly and feel connected to your organization's culture and values. Employers must invest in the success of new workers by creating intentional connections, clarifying expectations, providing training, and working to ensure that young adults starting their careers remotely receive the same level of support and feedback that they would receive in a traditional office environment.

The first ninety days

How to get new employees up to speed quickly? That's where the importance of the first ninety days comes in. In some businesses, the first three months is a probation period, a time that can often make or break a new employee's experience.

Here are my tips to help you set your new hires up for success:

- **Create an awesome onboarding plan:** Your plan should outline all the significant activities your new employees will need to tackle in those first few months. Think training sessions, orientation meetings, introductions to team members, and any other company-specific information that's essential to know. This will give new hires a clear understanding of what's expected of them and how to succeed in their new role.

- **Assign a work "best friend forever" (BFF):** Seriously, everyone needs a work BFF. And your new employees are no exception. Assign a coworker as a buddy to help them navigate the company culture, answer questions, provide support, and help them fit in culturally. This person should be their go-to resource for any and all concerns they might have (within reason). Having a work BFF can make all the difference in those first ninety days.

- **Reinforce expectations:** The first ninety days is when you must reinforce what you've already talked about in the interview process, which usually includes the role of the employee, their responsibilities, specific goals, and how they'll be evaluated. With a system in place to make sure they receive a lot of guidance and specific support in those first ninety days, you can turn that probation period from a time of anxiety to a positive experience.

- **Embrace innovative approaches:** Companies like Airbnb and Atlassian offer unique onboarding experiences. Airbnb focuses on cultural immersion, encouraging new hires to stay at an Airbnb listing to experience the company's core values firsthand. Atlassian, meanwhile, emphasizes teamwork and collaboration in its onboarding process, fostering a sense of community and encouraging new employees to work together and share knowledge.

We've explored the theories and strategies reshaping the workforce, but the real journey begins when we apply these insights. In Chapter 13, we transition from concepts to concrete actions, turning these foundational ideas into effective hiring practices.

Learning pods

Imagine small groups of employees from various departments uniting with a shared purpose of mastering new skills or concepts.

Take my son James, for instance. During the COVID-19 pandemic, he announced he was joining a new learning pod. "A what?" I asked. Styled on those emerging nationwide due to pandemic-induced school shutdowns, these pods each had four or five students, including my son, collaborating online and, when possible, in person. "Why this approach?" I wondered. James explained that these pods provided invaluable social and emotional support—a stark contrast to my own school days.

I must admit I was late to the learning pod party. But now, it's clear: why should kids have all the fun? Reframing workplaces as dynamic learning environments, where the daily grind morphs into an engaging, skill-building journey—that's a game-changer.

In these pods, everyone—from supervisors to managers—becomes a problem-solver, a troubleshooter. Employees are not just cogs in the machine; they're active learners, building competence and independence. These pods can pop up around specific projects or tasks, adapting to the ebb and flow of work. Staffers need not be tied to one pod all day; they navigate between them as their work demands evolve.

Let's say there's a unit of e-learning. Instead of isolating staff at their computers, why not bring them together? Let them debate, discuss, and truly own the learning process. Throw in a mobile learning app with quizzes and leaderboards, and you've turned a mundane task into a lively, memorable experience.

This concept isn't new. It's akin to Google's "Genius Hour," when employees dedicate time to passion projects. It's about professional development, building a learning community, and frankly, enjoying the work we do.

For instance, in a technology firm I visited, a learning pod was set up to explore AI. Employees from different specializations came together under this initiative, delving into AI's complexities with the guidance of an industry expert. Together, they embarked on a project that applied AI to a real-world problem faced by their company. This hands-on experience not only enhanced their technical expertise but also bridged gaps between departments.

Learning pods also serve a crucial role in offering social and emotional support in the workplace. These pods remind us that learning is not just an individual pursuit but a collective journey, in which each member contributes to and benefits from the shared experience. But perhaps the most exhilarating aspect of learning pods is the principle of learning by doing. This approach resonates deeply with me because I firmly believe in its effectiveness. When we engage in practical, hands-on projects, our learning becomes more dynamic and impactful. It's not just about absorbing information; it's about applying it, testing it, and seeing it come to life. This experiential process not only solidifies our understanding but also sharpens our skills, preparing us for the challenges and opportunities that lie ahead.

This learning-by-doing approach is something I stand by wholeheartedly. It's not just theoretical learning; it's applying, getting your hands dirty, and growing in real time. And it translates directly to tangible improvements and innovations in our work.

Unlimited time off

To attract and retain talented staff, companies are getting creative with perks such as "unlimited paid time off" (UPTO), as it's known in HR circles. The idea is simple: give your employees as much time off as they need for illness, personal reasons, or holidays. It's a perk that top-tier companies like Goldman Sachs and Microsoft adopted early to lure in new talent. And now, it's becoming the norm in 20 percent of US firms.[2]

But is UPTO really the quick fix it promises to be? Some employees have reported difficulties in taking time off, even with this benefit. They feel a sense of loyalty to their organization and their peers, and they can't bear the thought of the negative impact their absence might have. So whereas UPTO may sound like a great idea, it's worth considering the deeper implications before implementing it in your organization. You also need your workforce to understand that days off does not mean the work can be put aside. Remember: the workload will still be waiting for them upon their return.

But let's not just stop at UPTO. When we talk about work-life balance, we can't help but consider the growing body of research supporting a shorter workweek. For example, studies conducted in Iceland, involving a significant portion of their workforce, found that reducing work hours to about thirty-five or thirty-six hours a week, instead of the standard forty, not only maintained productivity but, in many cases, improved it. Employees reported a dramatic increase in well-being and work–life balance, with no decrease in service quality or output.

There are other innovative perks that companies are offering besides highly competitive salaries and healthcare packages, such as childcare reimbursements, fertility benefits, on-site fitness classes, housecleaning services, and even pet insurance. Yes, you read that right—pet insurance.

Let's not forget the lessons we can learn from the past. Take the Henry Ford approach, for example. He cut workers' hours to an unheard-of eight-hour workday and doubled their wages overnight. It sounds like a recipe for disaster, but it worked. Ford's staff turnover rate plummeted from 370 percent to 16 percent, and absentee rates dropped to 2 percent. But here's the kicker: Ford's approach was not just about reducing hours and increasing pay; it was part of a broader initiative that included improving employees' lifestyles, such as offering English lessons and promoting good character and living conditions. This holistic approach to employee welfare was revolutionary at the time. Ford was also trying to build a more affordable car, one which his employees could afford.

Perhaps it's time to refocus on the whole employee and their life outside of work. Research, including recent trials, suggests that reducing work hours can improve work–life balance and boost employee health and well-being. And it can be a more affordable and important health investment for all.

It's also important to keep in mind that whichever approach you take to revamping the workweek, don't create a two-tier system among your employees, one for managers and one for employees. Involve your employees in planning their benefits package to ensure it is meaningful to them. And most importantly, make sure your perks are focused on their needs. In the end, that will keep your employees happy, motivated, and loyal. And happy employees lead to happy, satisfied customers. And that will keep your ship sailing smoothly.

Retaining top talent

Many of the strategies we've discussed can significantly reduce employee turnover, a major cost for any business.

Here's how you can keep your top talent:

- **Set clear goals and expectations:** Ensure that every team member knows what's expected of them and what success looks like in their role.

- **Provide meaningful work:** Assign tasks and projects that are not only interesting but also challenge employees and contribute to their acquisition of new skills.

- **Recognize and reward good work:** Don't underestimate the power of a heartfelt thank-you. Acknowledge and appreciate the hard work your employees put in.

- **Foster a positive workplace culture:** Cultivate an environment where respect and support are not just words but actions that define your company culture.

- **Offer opportunities for learning and development:** Invest in your employees' future by providing them opportunities to learn new skills and advance their careers.

- **Give employees autonomy:** Trust your employees, and allow them the freedom to make decisions and take charge of their work while setting reasonable boundaries.

- **Get feedback from employees:** Regularly seek out their opinions and suggestions. Listen actively, and respond constructively. When feasible, implement changes that address their needs and concerns, thereby showing that their input truly matters.

Team building 2.0

From my experience managing a training and conference facility, I've seen firsthand the impact of both effective and lackluster team-building activities. The most successful ones were those that embraced creativity and truly understood the essence of teamwork.

However, team-building events are not always successful. I remember a particular one during which we embarked on a whitewater rafting adventure. The raft flipped, and suddenly, we were all in the water. At that moment, the only teamwork that mattered was ensuring that everyone was safe. Although it was a bit extreme and not everyone's cup of tea, it was a bonding experience we never forgot.

After our near brush with death, we decided to opt for a calmer activity next time. We found ourselves in a local restaurant's kitchen making soup dumplings together. It was a delightful experience, filled with laughter and chatter—a far cry from our adrenaline-filled rafting escapade. This culinary adventure allowed us to connect on a different level, sharing stories and experiences while crafting delicious dumplings.

Although I personally tend to steer clear of tight spaces, I can't ignore the buzz around escape room challenges (from young people in my world, anyway). They seem to be a hit for those who thrive under pressure and enjoy solving puzzles as a team. However, it's crucial to remember that team-building activities should cater to the comfort levels of all participants to be truly effective.

Team building centered on food has this incredible way of uniting people. It's more than just enjoying a meal together; it's about exploring different cultures, trying out new cuisines, and even sharing a laugh about culinary experiments gone wrong. After all, food is a universal language that everyone speaks.

For successful team building, it's best to steer clear of activities that might lead to embarrassment, discomfort, or over-the-top competition in which some might feel awkward or intimidated. Such experiences can create negative vibes and certainly won't encourage anyone to put forth their best effort. Instead, focus on activities that are familiar to most team members, ensuring there's no steep learning curve or significant skills gap. The goal is to foster unity, not division. Choose activities that bring your team together, creating a sense of camaraderie and collaboration in an environment that is comforting and where it is easy to communicate—which leaves bowling or Go-Karts out. You might also avoid anything involving weapons, including paintball.

With these insights, you're well equipped to create an environment where your employees feel valued, respected, and motivated. Remember: a united team is the backbone of any successful business, and your efforts in nurturing this unity, if planned correctly, can set your company apart.

CHAPTER 4

Let's Talk About the Next Generation

———

DURING HER FINALS EXAM, HIGH SCHOOL SENIOR EMILY encountered a math problem that asked her to calculate food combinations in a school cafeteria scenario.

Question: *If Madison could choose from two starters, three main courses, and three desserts, how many meal combinations could Madison choose from?*

Emily's answer: *"None. Madison has food allergies."*

The teacher, taken aback by this literal yet witty response, couldn't help but acknowledge the cleverness. This cheeky answer is more than humorous; it's possibly a testament to the unique perspectives the younger generation brings to the table.

This unexpected twist serves as a metaphor for the unprecedented waves of change sweeping through the American economy and workforce. This workforce transition demands different and more diverse solutions than previous generational shifts.

An HR manager once told me a story that perfectly illustrates the generational divide, about a younger employee's grievance against their manager's communication style. *What had they done?* I wondered. The manager was accused of old-school intimidation for picking up the phone and actually calling the employee—apparently, in the unwritten book of workplace etiquette, that's no longer assumed acceptable. I guess it's time to brush up on my emoji language! Curious, I probed further. Apparently, the employee preferred texting, in which edits could be made in the conversation as it unfolded. This is certainly a different take on workplace communication.

I ran into this myself in the office recently when I mentioned a "CD-ROM" during a meeting. The room went silent until one of the younger team members asked, "Nick, what's a CD-ROM?" Everyone burst out laughing, realizing the gap between our experiences. It was a stark reminder of how rapidly our work environment is evolving.

Give me a break; it's not like I asked where to insert the floppy disk or pulled out a flip phone.

Gen Z: here's what you need to know

Over two decades of leading a company that transitions young people from school to skill-based careers, I've come to appreciate and understand people through real conversations. My discovery is that young individuals, despite being tech savvy and preferring digital communication, also value personal relationships and direct, face-to-face interactions. So, in research for this book, I decided to do just that: I surveyed young people who recently joined the workforce. I wanted to understand their interests and thoughts on the new world of work.

After all, Gen Z now makes up 22 percent of the global population and 27 percent of the global workforce, signifying their major impact in the world today. But are you ready for a new generation to take over the workplace? Look no further than Gen Z. This dynamic cohort, born between 1997 and 2009, is approaching work and life in a way that's vastly different from previous generations. And with the oldest members of Gen Z now reaching their mid-twenties, they're poised to make a significant impact in the workplace.

Gen Zers are digital natives, having grown up entirely in an internet-centric world, and they're comfortable with technology in a way that's unparalleled by previous generations. Asking a Gen Z for tech support is like asking a fish about water: they just get it. Recently, I was struggling with a setting on my latest iPhone. I tried to find a solution to no avail. A young staffer walking past me in the office noticed and, with a cheeky grin, swooped in, saying, "Nick, may I?" She clicked a few times on the screen, and voilà, problem solved. She joked, "Consider this my good deed for the day!" It was a reminder of the tech fluency this generation brings to the table.

To attract Gen Z talent, workplaces must adapt by integrating digital collaboration tools, catering to their innate comfort with technology. This strategy directly aligns with the "attract" component of our framework. Additionally, to retain Gen Z employees, fostering a culture that values work–life balance and offers opportunities for career advancement is vital, reflecting their unique values and workplace expectations. In terms of development, you'll want to focus on continual learning and adaptability. These play into Gen Z's desire for personal growth and professional development.

As the percentage of Gen Z in the workforce continues to grow, it's essential to adjust office practices, remote policies, strategies, and training to the demands of this new generation, without excluding your senior team members. Keep in mind that while you look to educate Gen Z regarding how your business works, you can also learn from this young generation, even as a manager. And yet Gen Zers also need to adapt to the real world, which is different from the classrooms they so recently inhabited. You should expect that they will be ready to listen and learn from those who are familiar with the company's mission, history, and culture.

I recall from my research a conversation with a Gen Z professional named Janie, who graduated high school and during a school mock interview session ended up having a real interview with an architect for a legitimate job. This chance encounter led to an internship and a career in architecture. (As we noted earlier, along with talent, luck can be helpful.) In my conversation with her, I gained insightful perspectives on what drove her career choices and interest. She shared with me her admiration for an architectural firm that had initiated a company-wide sustainability project, a move that resonated deeply with her. In contrast to the perk-focused inclinations of previous generations, she expressed a strong preference for a workplace that prioritizes ethical practices and sustainable initiatives. She emphasized that for her and her friends, the allure of a job is how the organization aligns with their values, particularly regarding the environment and social responsibility. She described how, in her team discussions and meetings, the focus often extends beyond company benefits to the broader impact of the company's work, which is what drew her in.

This shift in priorities, as articulated by Janie, illuminates a fundamental change in the modern workforce—one where the pursuit of purpose, ethical engagement, and environmental responsibility are taking center stage. Her insights not only showcased how she is carving a distinct path in the corporate world but also underscored the growing importance for companies to adapt to these evolving values to attract and retain this new wave of talent.

Generational overview: understanding different ages

The Builders (<1946): Resilient pioneers of modern society

Baby Boomers (1946–1964): Influential in social justice and cultural change

Generation X (1965–1979): Antiestablishment and entrepreneurial

Millennials (1980–1996): Global outlook with housing and employment challenges

Generation Z (1997–2009): Resilient, education focused, and socially conscious

Generation Alpha (2010-2024): Expected to be tech savvy while shaped by global events[1]

I had another great conversation with a twenty-four-year-old, Fearghus, in which we discussed the aspirations behind his career choice. He told me that after graduating high school, his calling was not in traditional college coursework but in a hands-on, practical type of career. So he chose to start a four-year automotive apprenticeship program with a large Mercedes dealer, because he had a strong interest in mechanical technology and engineering. This opportunity was also about working with a team, learning supervisory skills, and finding a sense of belonging in a large company where he could see a clear career progression path. He told me his manager at the dealership was a great communicator who started each day with a quick briefing, assigning the day's work for all the technicians. Fearghus's story exemplifies the importance for younger workers of seeking meaningful, skill-building experiences that resonate with their personal and professional goals.

Is there any published research to back up my observations and conversations? I found some, such as a fascinating study by Roberta Katz, an anthropologist at Stanford University. She let the secret out that almost all Gen Zers she talked to actually prefer chatting face-to-face.[2] Yep, in person! It's not all about texts and DMs. Who knew?

I'm sure plenty of people would have thought the opposite. But when I decided to dive into some data, the picture became even more nuanced. Australian consultant and researcher Mark McCrindle reveals in his findings that Gen Z is a mosaic of individuals, each mastering the intricacies of today with an unprecedented nimbleness and digital savvy. More than mere numbers, his research showed this generation forms a vibrant tapestry, navigating twenty-first-century complexities with agility and digital fluency, a path partly paved but not entirely grasped by their predecessors.[3]

Young people are rewriting the rules of the game, living in a world where change is the only constant. McCrindle's work underscores such constant change, noting that this generation is expected to navigate through a dynamic life journey, with an anticipated eighteen different jobs across six careers and fifteen different homes throughout their lifetimes. Their flexibility and adaptability are key traits that set Gen Z apart. Additionally, the research underscores Gen Z's profound concern for ethical consumption and authenticity.

In thinking about the changing aspirations of the younger generation, I'm reminded of the pop singer Olivia Newton-John. She managed to blend personal passion with professional success and became a beacon of inspiration in our rapidly transforming world. An "Aus-merican" icon, Olivia's life was about more than her unforgettable, chart-topping hits and her iconic role in the cult classic movie *Grease*. Born in England, raised in Australia, and an Australian citizen by choice, Olivia resonated with audiences everywhere through her music and her stead-fast dedication to philanthropy and cancer research. Beyond her fame, she represented a harmony of personal passion and professional success, a blend immensely appealing to today's workforce seeking deeper ful-fillment in their careers. Her story is motivational, especially for young women navigating the complexities of their career paths.

At a recent career fair at a high school in Riverside County, California, I spoke to a group of young people who were working the booths. Among the group was twenty-three-year-old Nadine, who had strong opinions on the purpose of work. She said she was personally turned off by large corporations, those that humbly brag about their achievements. "That's why I'm here [at the career fair]. I chose to work for a nonprofit, helping students make the school-to-work transition," she said, adding that she wanted a job with an organization that had meaning and ultimately helped others. Good one, Nadine, a job with purpose and meaning. I like that.

Authenticity matters: networking 101

In my conversations with young people entering the workforce, a recurring theme is their emphasis on authenticity, which means being truthful about how you present yourself to other people. Young pro-fessionals are learning the value of one-to-one genuine interactions and seek work environments in which transparency and authentic communication are paramount. Whether it's an entry-level worker or a seasoned manager, honesty in relationships and interactions holds immense value. It's essential in building trust, fostering collaboration, and ensuring a thriving work environment. With this understanding, let's delve into why being authentic matters.

I've come to realize the irreplaceable value of genuine human interaction. Even as technology and AI revolutionize how we interact, the essence of true connection remains unchanged. I have explored this in detail with my friend Patti Hunt Dirlam, author of *The Power of Everyday Networking*. In fact, Patti's practical networking advice is based in the attitude and intention one brings to every interaction. For example, Patti believes authentic networking is not new—it just can't be faked. She also emphasizes a networking approach that's grounded in real relationships and self-awareness (being your best self).

According to her, here are three pivotal ways to network authentically:

- **Focus on quality over quantity:** It's not about impressing everyone or having the most connections or followers. It's about forging meaningful relationships with those who resonate with your values and interests. Engage in conversations where you ask genuine questions, and actively listen. As a manager of mine says, that's why we have two ears and one mouth.

- **Understand yourself:** Knowing your values, goals, strengths, and weaknesses is crucial. It's also crucial to know what you don't know, as in being aware of subjects in which you are not yet proficient. This self-awareness allows you to network in a way that leads to finding other people from whom you can learn.

- **Prioritize face-to-face interactions:** Despite the convenience of digital connections, nothing can replace the richness of in-person interactions. Attend events, meet potential partners over coffee, and have real conversations. Face-to-face interactions are the bedrock of authentic networking.

In the era of social media, when online appearances often over-shadow reality, there's a concerning trend towards prioritizing virtual "likes" over genuine connections. My take is that whether networking in person or via social media, we should strive always for authenticity.

Patti Hunt Dirlam further explains that authentic networkers have learned the value and benefits to personalizing their approach. We all come to networking from different starting points, and your personal approach is part of what makes your actions authentically *you*. Remember: you network with individuals, not groups. Take this as a little nudge to interact with people as human beings, not as electronic transactions. Always treat everyone and their time with respect. Do your research, and ask good questions.

Organically grown

To me, workplaces should be a melting pot of diverse ideas, not bat-tlegrounds for cultural ideologies. As I see it, we should aim for a middle ground where individuality and common goals can coexist. But have we gone too far? Possibly—in both directions. Yes, people often take both positions to the extreme, which brings me back to the importance of finding some middle ground. I believe that a healthy, productive workplace is one with a culture that encourages everyone to contribute and express opinions, which organically fosters mutual respect, inclusivity, teamwork, and striving for excellence.

When I speak of organic growth in workplace culture, I mean fostering an environment naturally conducive to comfort and produc-tivity rather than forcing it. Culture grows like a plant: nature does the work; you can't make it happen. A mandate can create resentment, and in a workplace culture, it can be toxic.

Compulsion often backfires, as illustrated by the tale of Ethan, a manager I knew, and his "safe space" initiative. Ethan, determined to create a work culture with a cornerstone proposition of everyone feeling safe at work (mentally and emotionally, that is), launched his own safe spaces campaign within his company. He felt this is what young workers expected in a modern workplace. He began starting all his team meetings with a speech about everyone's right to feeling safe at work, and he then switched the speech to a proposition and invitation that anybody feeling unsafe during the meeting could retreat to a designated safe space he had created in the office. Yes, he has petitioned management to create a room designated "the safe space" and labeled as such.

Initially, the concept appeared cutting-edge. "Another step forward," one worker exclaimed about the company's care for its workers. However, over time, starting every meeting with the same speech began to feel ritualistic and disingenuous for many. Ethan's well-intentioned effort to foster inclusivity quickly turned into a source of friction among his team.

Some labeled Ethan's repeated safe space reminders as mere tokenism and a waste of team time while another described him as leading a political-correctness-gone-mad, almost-cult-like personal agenda. Perhaps this is what happens when someone has an idea (even a good one) but doesn't know when to stop selling it.

The company intervened after several written complaints. Ethan's safe space was quietly repurposed back to a general-purpose meeting room. He was mortally offended, complained that the company was old-fashioned, and went on stress leave. Ethan's story serves as a cautionary tale: good intentions can sometimes backfire. You cannot mandate how people should think, feel, or, in the case of Ethan, tell them where they must go to feel safe.

Cracking the code

For the past two decades, I have led a business that connects young workers with companies. My team and I have made the connection and designed the programs, and in many instances, we've acted as the employer of record during the person's training.

This has given me valuable insights for engaging young workers:

- Keep younger workers on their toes with ever-evolving job roles that push the boundaries of skill development.
- Inspire younger workers to meet their potential with supportive supervision.
- Inspire by example.
- Involve workers in decision-making.
- Provide and invite constructive feedback, which can ignite your team's passion and enthusiasm.
- The secret ingredient? Engagement. It's not the case of a sprinkle here and there; it's the main seasoning.

Like many young people, Melissa freely acknowledges that after completing high school, she was uncertain about how to get started in her career. The problem was getting that first professional role: "I had a casual job at a retail store," she says, but she was seeking a career in business administration. However, without any experience in business, she was finding it difficult to land a full-time job in the industry she wished to join.

During her job search, the rejections began to dampen her enthusiasm. "I was living at home with my parents and lacking motivation," explained Melissa, who soon found and participated in a hands-on, learning-by-doing skills program. The program offered structured learning, related instruction, and fast-tracked her towards her goal. Melissa was placed at a leading bank for the on-the-job component of the program. Once she completed the program, the bank offered her ongoing employment. "This hands-on workplace-based program opened up a lot of doors. I've gained more confidence, and now I think I can do anything I put my mind to," added Melissa.

Melissa remembers being a nineteen-year-old having to make adjustments to her lifestyle. "I had to quickly balance my life." She went from being a high school student to being based at a site full of executives where she works on the same floor as the CEO. She was super nervous that she didn't have any experience, but she was paired with a workplace buddy who helped her settle into her new role.

A few months in, Melissa was taking on a wide range of responsibilities, including office management, assisting with payroll, and onboarding and training new employees—all part of a structured, twenty-four-month program.

Melissa's life has been transformed through her role: "Beyond the expanded responsibilities and self-confidence, I definitely feel secure professionally," she says. "It's been life-changing."

Melissa undertook what is known as an apprenticeship.

New chef job, big onions, and tears

I'll never forget the first day of my career (not the after-school hourly "jobs"). The HR manager's opening welcome was, "At our hotel, we value attitude as much as skills." Wow. Talk about a valuable early lesson to set the tone for my career. I felt like I was becoming part of a team as he emphasized the significance of striving for excellence and how the book he was about to give us would benefit our future careers. After an orientation on safety, key personnel, and hotel functions, it was time to don our chef whites. From the in-house laundry, I received my crisp white jacket, its ten buttons signifying my role as a line cook and apprentice. This moment wasn't just the start of a job; it was a profound lesson in workplace culture and the power of a supportive environment in nurturing talent. This early career experience mirrors the broader HR principle that a nurturing environment is not just beneficial but essential for talent to flourish—a lesson I carry into every aspect of my HR practice.

All of us first-day apprentices were welcomed to the kitchens by German Executive Chef Klaus Lemm, who proceeded to drop a giant bag of onions on our prep bench. "Peel them," he told us. So we began peeling. One apprentice proudly proclaimed he had a faster technique and soon outstripped the rest of us in onion-peeling prowess. I didn't know it was a competition. Another young apprentice just talked and talked and talked. Me, I just peeled onions. And when we finished that first bag, along came another. The whole day was onions and more onions and plenty of tears. The next day brought new assignments from Chef Lemm, who had keenly observed our progress. The talkative apprentice landed in the staff cafeteria. The speedy onion peeler? Off to the banquet kitchen for more peeling. As for me, I was assigned to the prestigious Le Restaurant. I realized the previous day's task was less about peeling onions and more seeing about how one approached a task. I simply followed the instructions and did the job I was asked to do. And so my journey as a young chef began, filled with countless more hours of onion peeling and many more tears.

As I recall those days of tireless onion peeling, the key lesson is evident: the foundation of a thriving professional's journey lies in the capacity to keenly observe, listen, and execute tasks with precision— qualities I now seek in every candidate I interview.

There is no question about the importance of quality orientations or of observing and assessing employee attitudes and work styles in the first few weeks. Employers should regularly review task assignments to gauge employee performance and align responsibilities with individual strengths. This focus on individual strengths and attentive observation was Chef Lemm's approach in the kitchen and exemplifies a principle that echoes beyond the culinary world. Chef Lemm was wonderful at storytelling to teach the young apprentices, often using reflections from his own journey and experiences. (He would go on to write a book with that exact name, *Culinary Reflections*.) It's a testament to the universal value of nurturing talent and recognizing potential, a theme we will see vividly embodied in Chapter 8 in the story of Porsche, a brand synonymous with precision and excellence.

The power of apprenticeship

I've long been a huge fan of apprenticeships. Apprenticeships aren't training programs; they're jobs. They're game-changers for companies and individuals. They bridge the gap between learning and doing. In the world of modern apprenticeships, it's not about hammer and nails anymore; it's about code and cloud. The toolbox has had a digital makeover!

For employers, embracing apprenticeships is about more than just filling a vacant position. It is about opening a path for talent to evolve in sync with the rhythm of your company. This is the marriage of knowledge and real-world application, in which learning is as authentic as it gets—on the job, solving real problems, and contributing to tangible outcomes.

Let me tell you about another apprentice, Amy, from Silicon Valley. Her story is like a modern fairy tale. After having two children, she took a break, embraced motherhood, and then decided to dive right back into the tech world with a bang, all thanks to an apprenticeship with Adobe. Engulfed in the world of coding and digital creation, Amy didn't just absorb knowledge; she contributed her voice and, in the process, reshaped her future. In this mentorship program, Amy wasn't just shown the ropes, taught the skills, or trained to be a cog in the machine; she was respected as a peer, as a mind brimming with potential.

And the apprenticeship became a launch pad to a career that resonated with her aspirations. Now a full-time software engineer, Amy embodies the synthesis of lifelong learning and professional zeal. Adobe's leap of faith in Amy was repaid with her unwavering commitment, exemplifying how when apprenticeships offer young (and sometimes older) professionals the tools to carve out their destiny, they don't just fill roles; they elevate them.

Apprenticeships are also programs that companies and governments can run at scale. My company has graduated more than 20,000 individuals into skills-based careers through apprenticeships. From automotive technicians and healthcare workers to IT and cybersecurity experts, each is able to take with them not only what they learned on the journey, but they also receive a nationally recognized qualification they will have for life.

In today's market, where technological advancement outpaces traditional educational methods, apprenticeships are the answer to the skilled labor shortage many sectors are experiencing. They are the crucial link between dynamic learning and workforce readiness.

In essence, apprenticeships are creating a skills pipeline to feed the future of your business. They're an opportunity to mold the workforce with precision, ensuring that every skill is honed, every potential is tapped, and every investment yields a return not just in productivity but in innovation and progress.

Apprenticeship vs. internship: what's the difference?

The terms "apprenticeship" and "internship" are often used interchangeably. How do you tell them apart? First, an internship is generally much more limited in scope than an apprenticeship. Internships are often unstructured and unpaid. Not all internships are like this, of course, and there are many valuable and rewarding internship experiences available; I'm simply speaking generally. In contrast, apprentices are paid to work and learn on and off the job. Apprenticeship programs include structured training designed to develop skills and knowledge in a specific trade or profession, en route to receiving a formal certification on completion of the apprenticeship.

A modern apprenticeship also augments the best components of career technical education (CTE), which combines hands-on job experience with classroom education, ensuring that participants not only get a job but also gain the skills and qualifications needed for a successful long-term career. Community college and CTE courses are valuable, but on completion, individuals still need to search for a job, whereas a successful apprenticeship typically leads to a full-time job, providing immediate work experience and a clear career pathway.

While internships provide general on-the-job experience, apprenticeships build a highly skilled and customized, steady flow of talent, preparing workers who typically stay around for the long term. This is backed up by data from the American Apprenticeship Initiative (AAI) by the US Department of Labor, which notes that 90 percent of apprentices who complete their program are employed and 65 percent are working for the same employer with whom they undertook their apprenticeship.

Some community colleges get it, like in my home state of California. They see the value in partnerships with companies and other employers on apprenticeship programs. But sadly, many colleges in other states don't see the value. In fact, they see apprenticeships as competition to their training programs.

As an employer, you might establish your own apprenticeship program. It involves a series of steps and careful customization, and although it's rewarding, it can be quite the undertaking. That's why engaging a technical expert can be a smart move. Look for individuals or firms with a solid track record in successfully setting up apprenticeship programs. With the right expertise on your side, you can structure a program that not only meets the immediate needs of your business but also paves the way for sustained growth and development.

If apprenticeships intrigue you, keep these tips in mind:

- Determine where your program will take place and what licenses or legal documents you may need to provide in your city, state, or country.
- Identify the occupation for apprenticeships. What skills are needed?
- Formulate and implement the program by engaging an internal team.

- Form external partnerships with high schools and community agencies.

- Select training providers.

- Identify mentors and coaches.

- Establish on-the-job training goals.

- Develop evaluation and feedback mechanisms.

- Define training and scalable wage structures and plans for progression.

- Understand legal and compliance obligations.

- Develop marketing and recruitment strategies to attract candidates.

A final inside tip on apprenticeship: federal spending on apprenticeships in the United States in recent years has jumped from roughly $30 million to more than $250 million per year. Although apprenticeship funding is still small compared with other Department of Labor (DOL) training allocations (Job Corps alone is at $1.7 billion) and the scale of US apprenticeships remains limited compared with that of other countries, apprenticeships have attracted widespread bipartisan support. And I have long expected government(s) to increase support to employers sometime soon. Apparently, my wish came true as I wrote this book: the DOL announced the availability of nearly $200 million in grants to continue to support public–private partnerships that expand, diversify, and strengthen registered apprenticeships. The DOL press release noted that the "funding opportunity includes $95 million of competitive grants through the second round of the Apprenticeship Building America Grant Program and $100 million in the second round of State Apprenticeship Expansion Formula Grants."

The DOL also pointed to some sectors where registered apprenticeships are in high demand:

- Information technology/cybersecurity
- K–12 teacher occupations
- Care economy (nursing, early childcare, mental health occupations)
- New energy
- Hospitality
- Public sector
- Supply-chain sectors (logistics, warehousing, transportation, manufacturing)

So you see, now is a great time for your company to join the apprentice jobs skills revolution. For more on apprenticeships, visit www.dol.gov.

CHAPTER 5

Good vs. Not-So-Good Leadership

———

IN MY EARLY CULINARY DAYS, MY BOSS, CHEF BRUCE, tasked me with finding a courgette. It's okay; I didn't know what it was either. So, not knowing what I was looking for and sure as heck not being able to pronounce it (core-zhet?), I went with gusto into the cold room full of produce without any clue what this mysterious veggie looked like. I then proceeded to grab one of each vegetable I saw for good measure. Returning triumphantly to the kitchen, I couldn't help but notice Chef Bruce's contorted face as he stared at my many assorted vegetables and proceeded in teasing amusement: "What are you making, Wyman? Juice?!" I gladly accepted some early career humiliation so everyone else could have a good laugh at my expense. We all have funny or embarrassing moments from our early jobs to look back on, stories of screwing up or simply being naive. (By the way, a courgette is a zucchini. I don't know why the British call it that.)

Working under the watch of Chef Bruce was never easy; any misstep I or my fellow apprentices made was met with a harsh rebuke. It was a form of tough love; he demanded excellence, emphasizing the setting of boundaries. Though I didn't appreciate it at the time, looking back now, I realize his approach was quite placid compared to with what I encountered later working in some of Europe's most renowned kitchens. These chefs demanded absolute respect and perfection from their kitchen brigades. It was a tightly controlled workplace, top-down management, and the boss chefs saw it as a good way to keep people in line and productive. They believed this because it's how they were brought up. It was a learned behavior, passed down from one generation to the next.

The truth is, this management style and its effects can be devastating on individuals. It stifles creativity, crushes morale, and leaves people with a bad taste in their mouths . . . even in a kitchen.

Today, the strict authoritarian management style has fallen out of favor in many places. It's a style known for rigid task expectations, stringent guidelines that must be followed precisely, and direct, often negative feedback. Rooted in a system of rank and role and more common (and necessary) in military settings than workplaces, such an approach tends to stifle creativity and curb employee motivation—elements crucial for a business's growth and dynamism.

So what works today? Positive reinforcement and constructive feedback. For example, instead of scolding a person for their mistakes or dishing out blame, it is more effective with today's workers to highlight areas for improvement and even turn negatives into positive learning experiences.

Recognition is also important to success in the modern workplace. Today's employees expect to be supported, making the role of a coach or mentor more significant than ever. Additionally, developing effective communication skills is as important, if not more so, than having the technical skills for a job role. With more people not only changing jobs but careers often, it's essential that all workers have transferable skills. Many workplaces teach technical skills that are relevant only to employees' current roles but leave out training in areas like communication and people skills.

Good leadership

Let's look at some winning styles of leadership. Good leaders

Consult:

- Ask and answer questions
- Allow all employees to feel heard and valued
- Boost team motivation and commitment

Involve:

- Include others in planning and decision-making
- Lead from within and by example
- Build a culture *with* employees, not *for* employees

Coach:

- Assess the talents of everyone involved, with a goal of boosting such talent
- Focus on individual development and growth
- Act as a mentor and provide support and guidance

Communicate well:

- Give praise when deserved
- Pay attention to what their team is saying (and not saying) about their work and anything else related to the business and/ or their needs
- Actively listen

Not-so-good leadership

Now that we've seen some aspects of good leadership styles, let's flip the coin and talk about the not-so-good side. Not-so-good leaders

Micromanage:

- Push people away (and many people leave the company)
- Lower levels of productivity and morale
- Lead to higher staff turnover
- Can damage a company's reputation

Fail to provide equal treatment:

- Can create division, which leads to favorites and disengagement from those who are not part of the "in-crowd"
- Shows biases or discrimination, which can lead to serious issues if the behavior is blatant

Vanish:

- Fail to lead by example
- Aren't accessible to employees
- Do not set up or stick to schedules

Communicate poorly:

- Do not provide clear instructions
- Do not provide critical feedback
- Lower enthusiasm and raise stress levels
- Fail to relay important news promptly and properly (*Oh, by the way, you're fired.*)

Job descriptions

At my company, we ditched the conventional job descriptions for a dynamic "what, when, and how" list after a person is hired. Let's be honest: who looks at their position description after they're hired? The "what, when, and how" list is a personal performance plan, refreshed annually for everyone, myself included. It sets clear, adaptable goals, charting the direction rather than micromanaging the journey—think regular check-ins and frequent (but not too frequent) one-on-ones.

And then, my advice is to get out of the way. Yes, of course, offer training and support, but don't ask the same question at the close of business each day. It generally drives people crazy. History has shown us time and time again the far-reaching consequences of bad managers (I'm sure you have had one). Impact can range from financial losses and reputational damage to a toxic work environment and low employee morale.

The saga of Uber serves as a stark reminder: small leadership lapses can snowball into major crises. From fostering a toxic culture to stirring up legal storms, ex-CEO Travis Kalanick eroded trust in the company's upper ranks, leading up to his departure in 2017. This cautionary tale exemplifies the fallout that can happen from ignored leadership flaws.

When it comes to performance issues, I like to ensure no surprises. If someone is underperforming, they shouldn't learn about it for the first time during a dismissal conversation. That's a hallmark of poor management. My approach involves giving each individual the opportunity to correct their performance. I like having documented, clear discussions about where the employee is falling short and what is expected of them. Setting unambiguous performance standards and providing regular, constructive feedback enables my team members to understand and meet these expectations.

Then there's Simon's story, one of my more eye-opening leadership moments. A finance manager with a knack for numbers, Simon struggled with team leadership. Through direct meetings and a tailored development program, he began to excel in managing his team. However, while focusing on one area, another faltered: his financial reporting slipped. This misstep didn't escape the attention of the auditors, who escalated it to the board. In a twist I didn't see coming, Simon overheard the auditors discussing his impending dismissal. Confronted with this, I had to navigate this sensitive issue head-on. It was a stark reminder that leadership isn't just about guiding; it's about clear communication and managing the fallout when things don't go as planned.

The high cost of negativity

"It's sedition. That's what it is!" During World War II, having a negative attitude wasn't just frowned upon; it was outright illegal. Under the Smith Act of 1940, talking down about the country in public would land you in jail for being "seditious." I'm not suggesting we throw every office pessimist in a cupboard, but it does show how seriously negativity was taken back in the day.

Do you have a negative Nancy in the workplace? Someone who always sees the glass as half empty? Perhaps this person rolls their eyes when you or others talk. Or maybe this person dominantly shuts down any potential solutions to challenging problems. You might have an employee who has some, or all, of these traits. Negative people waste so much time and energy, and that saps the resources of those who have to listen to them, too.

What if we could redirect that energy? Instead of allowing constant negativity to block progress, imagine channeling it into finding positive outcomes. Shift the mindset from automatically saying no to exploring how.

Early in my culinary career, the chef managers you met earlier had no time for such pessimism and would respond brutally to negative talk: "If I wanted your opinion, I would have asked for it!" Take that. Although this might not work so well nowadays for many reasons, there are several constructive ways of addressing negative people and their disruptions.

Ignoring issues such as someone constantly bad-mouthing the company, being overly assertive, dominating meetings and conversations while claiming all ideas as their own . . . that helps no one—it's bad for you, the team, and the whole company. I understand that managing a team can be tough, but being an indecisive manager or trying to please everyone and ending up pleasing no one makes the job that much more challenging.

I use a metaphor with my managers and team when facing an issue that needs to be resolved. Consider the following scenario. We are at a T-intersection, and you have two choices: you either turn left towards positivity or right to negativity. There is no option to continue straight ahead. Whatever you call it, the key is to nip it in the bud.

Here are a couple of other tools to consider. The first is the "above and below the line" model. More traditional HR people I know use this model, developed in the 1990s by leadership experts Connors and Smith. "Above the line" represents positive, solution-oriented, and accountable behavior, fostering a collaborative and productive work environment. Conversely, "below the line" encompasses negative and unproductive behavior, including negative talk and a sour outlook. This model, simply put, is having a tough but constructive conversation with employees to understand the root cause of their negativity and guide the employee towards more positive and productive behavior.

For a slightly different approach on how to view this challenge, let's dive into Dr. Cameron Seth's performance values matrix. Picture a grid split into four: "Competent Nice Folks," "Incompetent Nice Folks," "Competent A-Holes," and "Incompetent A-Holes." Since we've established our problem isn't about the nice folks, we're looking at the other two quadrants. If someone is dragging down both morale and performance (their own or the company's), they are squarely in the "Incompetent A-Hole" zone. Dr. Seth's prescription? Fire fast. But if they're delivering results while being negative or steamrolling over everyone's spirits, we are in "Competent A-Hole" territory. Here, the approach is to remediate or separate. It's about giving them a chance to realign with company values, but with a clear ultimatum: shape up or ship out.

Dr. Seth points out a common pitfall in many organizations: the tendency to retain "Competent A-Holes." Why? Because they're often viewed as indispensable or too challenging to replace. But this is a critical error. By keeping these individuals around and not addressing the negativity, a company inadvertently endorses their negative behavior. It's like giving them a free pass to act out just because they deliver results. This not only undermines the company's values but also sends a dangerous signal to the rest of the team: that as long as you're valuable enough, you can bend the rules. It's a slippery slope and can erode the integrity of the workplace, creating a culture where respect and cooperation take a back seat to performance.

Regardless of whether you use these models or something else, the key is to have a conversation. Let the employee know that you sense negativity, or whatever the behavioral issue you seek to address, without blaming them or making accusations. You need to explain the behavior without antagonizing them. Use a specific workplace example, and explain how it is impacting the company and other employees. Responding to a negative comment might be as simple as asking, "Are you okay?" This generally causes people to pause and ask, "Why?" And you can lead the conversation from there. You can state politely, "I thought you might be upset about something." That's not an accusation; it's simply your impression of the situation.

Hopefully, the conversation will make them feel more positive about the company and their work. There's no guarantee this will work, but often, people are happy to be heard or to simply know that you took the time to talk with them. However, if the problem is outside of your jurisdiction or control—meaning they are negative for other reasons—a little empathy can go a long way. Jamie Dimon, CEO of JP Morgan Chase, demonstrates a unique approach to accessible leadership. Each Friday morning, he sits on a bench in the lobby of the company's New York City headquarters. Any employee can join him to ask a question, share an idea, or have a conversation. This simple gesture underscores the power of direct, open communication in fostering trust and connection between leaders and employees. By being approachable and empathetic, Dimon exemplifies how even small acts of accessibility can create a more positive and engaged workplace culture.

CHAPTER 6

Safety and Integrity

———

WHILE STANDING UNDERNEATH THE RETIRED AIR FRANCE Concorde F-BVFA at the Smithsonian's Steven F. Udvar-Hazy Center at Dulles Airport, in Washington, D.C., I was in awe of this supersonic jet; it wasn't just an engineering feat but a narrative of human ambition and innovation.

It also made me think of Barbara Harmer, who, in a striking example of career transformation, went from being a hairdresser to becoming the world's first female Concorde pilot. Her journey showcases the incredible potential for skill development within the aviation sector and proves that with the right training and opportunities, individuals can transition from seemingly unrelated fields into highly skilled technical roles. The difficulty of becoming a pilot emphasizes the aviation industry's commitment to safety and skill development, and rigorous training and precise expertise are crucial. The sector not only values but necessitates continuous learning and personal advancement yet recognizes that talent can come from the most unexpected backgrounds.

The Concorde, a product of Franco-British collaboration from the 1970s, symbolized more than technological advancement; it was a dream of international cooperation. Capable of crossing the Atlantic in less than three hours, its legacy is more than speed; it's a testament to the spirit of ingenuity and collaboration.

However, the Concorde's story isn't without its darker chapters. In 2000, Concorde Air France Flight 4590 was ready to take off. As it sped down the runway at Charles de Gaulle Airport, it hit a titanium metal strip that had fallen from the engine of a Continental Airlines DC-10 just ten minutes earlier. Measuring only the length of a school ruler, the strip caused a tire on the Concorde to burst. The resulting debris struck the wing, creating a shock wave in the fuel tank, leading to a massive fuel leak and a devastating fire. Unable to gain altitude or speed, the damaged Concorde crashed just ninety seconds after takeoff, claiming 113 lives.

In 2000, Concord Air France Flight 4590 crashed 90 seconds after taking off from the Charles de Gaulle airport in Paris.

Contributing factors to this disaster included failure to follow tarmac inspection protocols, vulnerabilities in the Concorde's fuel tank design, and flawed maintenance practices with the use of a nonstandard, improperly secured part on the DC-10.

The aftermath brought about major changes in aircraft tire and fuel tank safety standards, along with revised maintenance and inspection protocols. The tale serves as a somber reminder that in the realm of aviation, the margin for error is small, and the consequences of oversight can be monumental.

Let's now turn to a brighter chapter in aviation. Imagine flying from New York to London in half the time it takes now. Boom Supersonic is reviving the golden era of supersonic travel with twenty-first-century safety and sustainability goals.

Named the Overture, the aircraft will fly at twice the speed of today's airliners and is designed to run on 100 percent sustainable aviation fuel. This isn't just an aspiration. Boom is now building a "super factory" in South Carolina that will have the capacity to produce up to thirty-three Overture aircraft per year.

It's worth noting that as futuristic as this all sounds, Boom's ambitions are materializing into real jobs—some of which never existed before. The factory will be home to a burgeoning workforce of engineers, pilots, data scientists, climate experts, and digital marketing specialists. However, while Boom's ambitions soar, they face real-world challenges like regulatory complexities and environmental impact concerns. This endeavor aims to break existing speed records, but it must still navigate the intricate realities of modern aviation.

While the Concorde may rest as a museum relic, its spirit continues to inspire. It serves as a stepping stone for the new wave of aviation technologies and the many opportunities it will bring.

Technology's role in a safer workplace

Beneath the bustling streets of New York City, a monumental project largely unknown to the city's residents unfolds: Water Tunnel No. 3. Initiated in 1970, it's now in its sixth decade, with a mission to supply clean drinking water to the residents of New York City and neighboring areas. That's generations of workers on the same project!

If you think that sounds like it's taking a long time, the Spanish Basilica Church in Barcelona has been under construction since 1882 and is now entering its 140th year! (All good things take time in Spain.) It's expected to be completed in 2026.

Barcelona's Basílica de la Sagrada Família has been under construction since 1882.

Water Tunnel No. 3, the crown jewel of New York City's infrastructure projects, is an engineering feat that exemplifies the transformative impact of technology on worker safety. The sixty-year span of its construction has not been without its share of darkness. Twenty-three lives were tragically lost, mostly in the early years. This stark reality served as an urgent call for change. From the mid-90s onward, the narrative has thankfully shifted: no more fatalities. The transformation came about thanks to embracing technology and automation. Tunnel boring machines (TBMs) began shouldering the most dangerous tasks, significantly reducing human risk. Training the workforce has also been a key part of the increased safety of the project. Water Tunnel No. 3 is expected to be completed in 2032.

Speaking of using technology to increase safety, the Basílica de la Sagrada Família's engineers have installed sensors to alert them to changes in the building's structure. It's an incredible building that you should check out if you are ever in Barcelona.

The harsh truth is that every accident, every close call, carries the same message: something could have been done differently. It's a reminder that safety isn't a checkbox; it's an ongoing commitment, a culture that needs nurturing.

Don't sweat the small stuff

Walking down the hallway of the mining company's global HQ where I worked at the time, morning latte in hand, I suddenly felt like I'd stepped into a sitcom. A figure dashed towards me, her footsteps echoing in the corridor. "Stop!" she yelled. *Who? Me?* It was the HR manager, her face stern, eyes fixed on my lidless cup. "Don't you know about our safety policy!? All hot beverages must have a lid!"

I was taken aback. The scene reminded me of the *Seinfeld* episode in which Kramer got burned by hot coffee, a riff on the real-life *Liebeck v. McDonald's* lawsuit. In this instance, this particular HR manager had one of those extreme, easily excitable personalities. In any case, there I was being ripped over a coffee lid in an office, while the previous year, sixteen people lost their lives at work in the very same company. And none of the incidents involved coffee. These were people being squashed between locomotives, washed off ships, and even one murdered in a mining camp.

There is no question: the mining industry has inherent dangers. Historically, mining tragedies like the Senghenydd Colliery Disaster of 1913 in Wales, which resulted in the deaths of 439 miners, were common. It's good to know that things have changed over the last hundred years. Sadly, fatalities and serious injuries are still happening in workplaces every day.

Ask yourself, *would you work for you?*

Reflecting on the above question is more than just a thought exercise; it's a critical assessment of your own workplace safety culture. This self-assessment is the first step in building a robust safety culture, a concept that the agency Worksafe highlights through its best practice ideas.

It's recommended that leaders:

- Identify hazards and act quickly to fix them before they become a risk to physical or mental health
- Find safer ways to work
- Show commitment to safety by complying with workplace health and safety (WHS) duties
- Prioritize and respond to safety-related issues or concerns
- Have regular talks with their team about safety matters and encourage everyone to report unsafe work or workplace hazards

- Break down barriers to reporting, such as fear of retaliation
- Promote a safety culture by displaying targeted safety information and/or installing guides and reminders in high-risk areas

It's an employer's responsibility to protect the company's workers and provide an orientation, plus training and information they need to work safely. I strongly recommend your company keep abreast of its duties and obligations as an employer at both federal and state levels. Of course, employees also have to take safety measures in whatever work they are personally doing. Watch for people who are not using safety measures, such as wearing protective goggles when necessary.

Diversity washing: when companies talk the talk but don't walk the walk

The corporate world's growing recognition of diversity and inclusion faces a serious challenge: "diversity washing." This is where genuine initiatives are overshadowed by superficial gestures and PR bluster.

It's quite revealing when companies ignore diversity completely or relegate it to a public relations checkbox. On occasion, this leads to something I find particularly grating: the corporate humblebrag. You know the type: companies that give modest grants to NGOs and then orchestrate a PR extravaganza, patting themselves on the back as if they've single-handedly saved the world.

For every corporate social responsibility (CSR) misstep and every instance of humble bragging, there are real champions of change making a significant impact. Jennifer McCrea, for example, through her program Exponential Fundraising, delivers this in spades. I connected with Jennifer at a conference in Athens with the Stavros Niarchos Foundation (which has committed $3.7 billion in grants worldwide).

We were there looking for solutions to the staggering 60 percent youth unemployment in that region. She told me that the money from a funder should be seen as "fuel in the tank rather than buying the car." It's a lesson in authentic support. This philosophy aligns perfectly with real CSR, in which the focus is on partnership and empowerment, not control or self-promotion.

Equally troubling is "greenwashing," in which firms boast eco-friendly policies for show, yet their real environmental impact tells a different story. It's like a car manufacturer claiming low emissions while secretly rigging tests. Then there's "pinkwashing," in which companies flaunting support for LGBTQ+ rights during Pride Month are found to be lacking substantive policies or year-round commitment. These practices aren't just misleading; they're betrayals of consumer trust.

However, companies should heed their stakeholders' preferences. A survey reveals that 77 percent of consumers prefer to buy from companies committed to making the world a better place, and 73 percent of investors consider a company's social and environmental efforts in their investment decisions. Clearly, good CSR equals good business.

Companies have recognized the benefits of having a diverse workforce, including increased creativity, innovation, problem-solving abilities, and financial performance. However, the shadow of diversity washing looms large, with companies making grand declarations of diversity but failing to implement meaningful changes.

A quick note on ESG vs. CSR: they're similar but distinct. ESG, which stands for environment, social responsibility, governance, is about measurable impacts. CSR is broader, looking at how a company positively impacts society. Both are vital to running an ethical business.

Abroad, some companies are getting it right. For example, consumer goods company Unilever in Europe isn't just talking diversity; they're actually doing it. They have committed to spending $2.4 billion annually on diversity and equality initiatives. Their goal is to create new employment models, provide essential skills to 10 million young people by 2030, and ensure that everyone involved in their supply chain earns at least a living wage by that same year.

For many small-to-medium-sized enterprises, real change starts with action. This can come in many forms, such as partnering with local schools, creating internships, and celebrating diversity openly. Moreover, the drive for change is not just external. According to *Harvard Online*, an overwhelming 93 percent of employees are looking for purpose in their work, and 95 percent assert that businesses should benefit all stakeholders, not just shareholders. Additionally, 88 percent believe it's no longer acceptable for companies to make money at the expense of society at large.

A disconnect between a company's public image and its actual workplace practices undermines the genuine efforts needed to bring about real change. As a workforce consultant, I have had companies contact me to talk about engaging people with disabilities, but the contact came from the public relations department of the organization.

Johnny C. Taylor, Jr., CEO of the Society of Resource Management (SHRM), hits the nail on the head: it's high time for businesses to move from token gestures to real action in diversity and inclusion. He's talking about a complete strategic overhaul to make diversity, equity, and inclusion (DEI) initiatives truly effective.

A broken moral compass

In the United Kingdom, local post offices are vital community hubs, typically run by small, trusted business owners, the subpostmasters. But this trust was shattered when Fujitsu's Horizon IT system was launched to modernize the post office.

The software, intended to streamline operations, generated false shortfalls in the accounts of thousands of subpostmasters, making it appear as if money was missing from the post offices. These people were suddenly and wrongfully painted as criminals. The most horrifying aspect? Fujitsu knew, and yet they let it happen. They watched for more than a decade (1999 to 2015) as people were jailed, some took their own lives, and others went bankrupt. When questioned at a recent inquiry, a Fujitsu director admitted, "My gut feeling would be yes," acknowledging the company's awareness of the Horizon system's problems for fourteen years. This isn't just a failure; it's a moral catastrophe. Fujitsu's executives themselves at the same inquiry noted that "there is a moral obligation for the company to contribute." They're absolutely right. It's not just about money; it's about accountability for human suffering.

Fujitsu, once known for technological reliability, now sees its reputation in ruins. The scandal sliced more than $2.4 billion off its market value. Greater than the final costs, this scandal will likely create a loss of trust and may lead to hesitancy or reluctance from potential and current partners to engage in future collaborations or contracts.

The truth always comes out

Following the stark revelations about Fujitsu, it's clear that corporate misconduct isn't just a blip on the radar. It's a systemic issue that demands our attention. I would be surprised if you were not aware of the companies on the following table, and most people know them for these scandals.

CSR is more than scandal avoidance; it's fundamentally about proactive safety and ethics. It's not enough to avoid being on the wrong side of the news; companies must actively work to do right by their employees, customers, and the environment. Now, let's look at a few infamous cases in which companies spectacularly failed in their CSR:

Company	Incident	Consequences
Volkswagen	Emissions scandal	Cheated on emissions tests; $30 billion in fines; environmental impact
Pepsi	Kendall Jenner Black Lives Matter (BLM) ad	Accused of trivializing the Black Lives Matter movement; ad pulled amid backlash
Facebook	Cambridge Analytical scandal	87 million users' data misused; $5 billion fine; trust erosion
Purdue Pharma	Opioid crisis role	Aggressive opioid marketing; more than 200,000 deaths linked; billions paid in settlements
Enron and Arthur Andersen	Accounting fraud	Enron bankruptcy; $74 billion lost; Arthur Andersen dissolved; 85,000 jobs lost
BP (British Petroleum)	Deepwater Horizon spill	Eleven deaths; largest marine oil spill on record; $65 billion in costs
Wells Fargo	Fraudulent accounts scandal	Created 3.5 million unauthorized accounts; $3 billion fine; trust erosion
Boeing	737 MAX safety issues	346 deaths in plane crashes; grounded fleet; more than $20 billion in costs
Equifax	2017 data breach	Exposed date of 147 million people; $700 million settlement
Monsanto (Bayer)	Roundup cancer lawsuits	Glyphosate linked to cancer; $10 billion paid in settlements
Uber	Workplace and privacy scandals	Sexual harassment allegations; 2016 data breach affected 57 million users

Analyzing effective CSR models

Contrasting the disheartening tales of Fujitsu and others are companies aiming high in CSR. Yes, ethical conduct and corporate success can go hand in hand. And no, you don't have to be a billion-dollar company to make a significant impact.

Here are a few companies, big and small, doing interesting things:

- **LEGO Group:** Committed $400 million to sustainability efforts, including the creation of eco-friendly "BioBricks" and setting up a carbon-neutral plant.

- **Warby Parker:** Their "Buy a Pair, Give a Pair" program partners with nonprofits, and they've distributed more than 15 million pairs of glasses.

- **Intrepid Travel:** This small-sized Australian adventure travel company has set ethical guidelines for content partners to represent diverse communities, including BIPOC, LGBTQIA+, and Indigenous voices. They are committed to ethical travel and cultural representation.

- **East Fork:** This North Carolina-based ceramics company has set a minimum wage well above industry standards, champions diverse talent recruitment, and actively contributes to local community organizations.

Good CSR is about making the right choices, day in and day out, and understanding that in business, just as in life, doing good is as important as doing well. And then there is ruthless and unscrupulous financier Gordon Gekko from the film *Wall Street*. Right before comparing the United States to a "malfunctioning corporation," he says, "Greed, for lack of a better word, is good." Sadly, in some cases, things haven't changed. Fortunately, in other cases, they have.

Sorry, Gordon: my moral compass points true north.

Part II

THRIVE

Empathetic cultural shift
Engagement and trust
Learning-driven environment

CHAPTER 7

Explorations of Life:
New Lessons Learned

———

THIS CHAPTER FOCUSES ON LEARNING EXPERIENCES, mostly my own, since I know them well. The essence of these pages is to illustrate how a variety of experiences can help you view the world, life, and the workplace differently. The stories I share are intended to make you think, occasionally laugh, and perhaps even roll your eyes. The point is simply that your experiences will help you create a richer work culture and environment, as mine did for me.

It's likely that you will relate not necessarily to the specific details of my stories but how I learned from them and from the people with whom I interacted. Whatever reactions I had in the moment, from wide-eyed amazement to wondering what the hell was going on, I took in so much from these encounters, and I hope my stories regale you as well as provide food for thought. Heck, I was a chef; I'll always work "food" in somewhere.

Old concepts revisited

Creating a positive workplace culture isn't rocket science. It's more like vegetable gardening—you plant seeds of respect, nurture them with collaboration, and sometimes, weed out the negativity. This is the essence of the New Work concept: cultivating a culture that blooms into a fruitful crop of productivity and success.

The New Work concept champions innovation, collaboration, and flexibility, reshaping traditional workplace dynamics. Although it may seem like a relatively modern concept, its origins actually date back to the 1970s, when Frithjof Bergmann, a German-born philosopher, introduced the theory.

Bergmann's ideas radically transformed traditional work structures. Championing individual fulfillment and creativity, he believed that every individual should find work that aligns with their values, desires, dreams, and skills, which would lead to personal fulfillment and autonomy in the workplace. His original concept was based on three pillars: freedom, self-determination, and community. Despite initial resistance to his ideas, Bergmann's thinking eventually gained traction in academic circles, particularly in Europe.

In this light, I recently connected with Håkan Lutz, CEO of Luvly, a company revolutionizing urban mobility with its innovative Light Urban Vehicle (LUV) concept. Luvly specializes in creating compact eco-friendly vehicles designed for city use, embodying efficiency and sustainability. Lutz shared, "In cities, it's increasingly obvious that traditional cars are now too big, too dirty, and too dangerous for pedestrians and other road users. The Luvly solution enables third-party producers worldwide to create their own versions of our LUV concept, which is greener and safer for society than cars and vans, but also more efficient and affordable."[1] This statement underscores the imperative of innovation and adaptability in today's work and technology culture. Lutz's vision of a sustainable, user-friendly urban mobility vehicle reflects a commitment to these ideals, demonstrating how embracing new ideas can lead to groundbreaking solutions.

John, Paul, George, Ringo, Sigmund Freud, and my dad

My father, a psychologist, found a kindred spirit in Bergmann's ideas. Like Bergmann, he believed in fulfilling work and giving people greater control over their work schedules. His unique perspective and style set him apart from the mainstream. As a child, I went with him on study tours to places like Sigmund Freud's house in Vienna, where my father once surprised me by climbing over the red ropes and sitting on Freud's toilet with his trousers on, explaining that "this is where the great man did his most profound thinking, and I wanted to derive inspiration." Being the son of a psychologist had its challenges, but it also exposed me to unique perspectives and experiences.

One of the things my father researched was the Beatles' 1964 Australia tour. He surveyed young people about their views at the time, gleaning fascinating insights into the behaviors of young people and generations. This sparked my interest in understanding generational drivers, a concept aligning with New Work's focus on personal fulfillment and creativity. It's interesting to think about how some of the ideas behind New Work, like collaboration, creativity, and personal fulfillment, might have also resonated with the young people my father surveyed. The Beatles' allure, transcending their music, mirrored young Australians' desire for change and self-expression, embodying the transformative spirit of that era. This enthusiasm for the Beatles represented a generational shift towards valuing creativity, individuality, and a break from traditional norms—echoes of which are seen in today's New Work philosophy. Just as the Beatles were challenging and reshaping the music industry, young people of that era were beginning to challenge and reshape their own roles in the workforce. They sought careers that were not just a means to an end but an expression of their identity and passions. This aligns closely with Bergmann's principles of freedom, self-determination, and community. The Beatles phenomenon, as observed by my father, underscored a pivotal change in societal attitudes. It highlighted a collective yearning among the youth to connect with their inner values in how they dressed, behaved, and even where they worked. The same concept is now more relevant than ever in our current discussions about the future of work.

Although some of the principle around New Work were considered too abstract sixty years ago, the underlying concept of leaving the world in a better place is worth embracing. Bergmann, my father, and other early pioneers believed in this concept, and their ideas and beliefs about work still inspire us today. The pandemic served as a catalyst, reawakening interest in long-standing theories and driving their application in today's workplaces. Not unlike fashion, old theories can come back into style.

Adaptability and many birds

Reflecting on the dynamic nature of New Work and its emphasis on adaptability and personal fulfillment, I think back on my work at the Gleneagles Hotel in Scotland. This experience was more than a mere culinary adventure; it was a real-world application of these principles. Nestled amidst Scotland's expansive landscapes, the Gleneagles Hotel, known for its luxury and historical significance, became a training ground for me, where I picked up invaluable lessons in adaptability, resilience, skill development, and teamwork.

Originally built in the Roaring Twenties, the hotel underwent a significant transformation during World War II, serving as a hospital for the wounded. As the war ravaged Europe, Gleneagles, a symbol of peace and luxury, closed its doors to the public in 1939 and embraced its new role in service of the nation. The corridors, once filled with the echoes of affluence and merriment, were now lined with beds holding injured soldiers. The war demanded that industry, particularly coal mining, step up. Miners, often overlooked as the backbone of the wartime economy, faced hazardous conditions underground, leading to numerous injuries. Gleneagles adapted to these exigencies and extended care beyond military personnel to treat these vital workers as well, transforming into a rehabilitation center for miners. This period was a testament to the hotel's resilience, repurposing its luxury for healing and recovery.

Following the war, Gleneagles transitioned back to a hotel, officially reopening its doors to guests in 1950. A few decades after that, I landed a job there as a *chef de partie*. For me, Gleneagles was a step up the culinary ladder and a master course in the complexities of leadership and teamwork. Contrary to the fancy French job title, my job wasn't about partying, though living in the hotel setting did offer its fair share of after-hours socializing. My job was to ascertain a good overall understanding of kitchen operations.

Stepping into the Gleneagles Hotel for the first time marked the start of one of the most exciting journeys of my life. This was more than just my workplace; it was to be my home. There were separate accommodations for male and female employees. The male staffers were housed in a basic temporary dormitory erected for a golf tournament years earlier. The water was often rather cold for a shower, as the heating didn't work, and the rooms were more like six-feet-by-eight-feet cells. To get from the dormitory to the hotel in winter, you would have to skate (or slide) across the icy car park. My first week at Gleneagles was quite the adventure, starting with a banquet featuring grouse, a game bird.

As I entered the kitchen, I was greeted by baskets of recently deceased birds, compliments of none other than Scottish Formula 1 racing legend Jackie Stewart, who had just returned from a morning hunt. Jackie had a shooting school at the hotel. My job was to prepare these birds for a gala banquet for the Royal Bank of Scotland that evening. The good news was the birds at least arrived already plucked, courtesy of skilled gamekeepers. But before the basting could begin, a delicate operation took precedence—the extraction of buckshot. So with tweezers in hand, I needed surgeon-like precision to find any tiny metal intruders in each bird. That took me hours and hours. Then, just before the evening meal service, Head Chef Alan Hill threw me a new white jacket and apron and yelled, "You'll need this, Mr. Wyman, it's time to meet the guests and join an ode to the haggis." I donned the crisp new jacket and was handed a sizable silver platter crowned with a large silver cloche (a domed cover to keep food warm and add an air of theater to food presentation). Underneath that cloche lay the celebratory haggis, a dish not to everyone's taste, made from finely chopped sheep's offal, adorned with onions, fat, oatmeal, and spices. Chef Hill's instructions to me were straightforward: smile, raise that haggis high above my head, and join the procession that would weave through the grand ballroom. I was flanked by a Scottish bagpipe player and a barman twirling not one but two bottles of Scotland's finest Scotch. (I was told one bottle contained scotch for the piper while the other had tea for the barman and me to join the toast; after all, we were on duty.) The task appeared straightforward. Key word: *appeared*.

As I entered the candlelit ballroom, I saw a crowd of glowing faces and people dressed in beautiful gowns, dinner suits, and kilts. It was at that point a realization struck me: this tray of haggis was damn heavy. I mean, really heavy. Unbeknownst to me, the silver presentation platter bore the ceremonial haggis, but concealed underneath a white napkin was a pile of kitchen scale weights: indeed, a cheeky welcome from the Scottish kitchen team to the new Aussie chef. With the procession now in full swing, the piper belting out "Scotland the Brave" on his bagpipes, the platter's weight quickly took center stage. I was struggling with the gravity. The spirited piper, his voice thick with a deep Scottish accent, stopped his bagpiping occasionally, yelling at me, "Lift it up, laddie! Higher, laddie!" Laughter rippled through the room. After a full lap around the room, we arrived at the stage to complete the culmination of tradition and celebration. The "ode to the haggis" was recited with flair by the piper. With the ode done, a shot glass was handed to me, and with a loud cry, the piper proclaimed a toast: "To the haggis!" The room erupted in cheers and the clinking of glasses. But lo and behold, my glass was not tea; it was pure Scotch whiskey. The piper winked. A toast to the haggis it was indeed. Now, a little tipsy, it was back to the kitchen for me—to plate up the grouse, haggis, and a strange dish called cranachan, a mixture of whipped cream, more whiskey, honey, fresh raspberries, and toasted oatmeal.

Later that evening, I returned the weights to the pastry shop and, for the first time, met a man who would become a mentor. Ian Ironside was the head pastry chef of twenty years. Drawn by tales of the Australian work ethic, he extended an open invitation to join him anytime in his pastry shop.

Chef Ironside was an unusual-looking, gnome-like man with a distinctly trimmed goatee and tiny spectacles perched atop his head. Living in the hotel with little to do in the winter months, I would find myself back in the kitchen learning the art of sugar pulling from a world master. One evening with Chef Ironside, we meticulously pulled and crafted fifty delicate sugar roses for a wedding cake. Chef Ironside's experiences were interwoven with the British culinary scene of the time, at one stage working for the Roux brothers, who were hailed as the godfathers of modern restaurant cuisine in the United Kingdom. They were credited with elevating British gastronomy through innovative techniques and culinary excellence. (Their recipe for *tarte au citron*—a legendary lemon tart—is especially memorable and worth looking up.)

I was soon moved to the pastry shop for three months. It was there that the firm yet fair Ironside insisted I delve into all aspects of a pastry shop, and that led to me finding myself relegated to the night bakery kitchen, a shift that began at the stroke of midnight. On my first night shift, I stood with the two wise old bakers adorned in flour-covered white singlet tops, trousers, and caps. The first few hours began with making the dough and then kneading and shaping it. As we gathered around a central workbench, I observed these old-timers' mastery of dough-working techniques, gained from years of practice. What made their technique somewhat unusual? Instead of rolling the dough into bread rolls on the bench, they formed the round roll shape on their chests. Two at a time. Yes, you read that right. The motion of shaping dough took on a whole new dimension. By 5 a.m., the dough was nestled in the ovens, and the vast pastry kitchens had the scent of freshly baked bread, heralding a new Scottish dawn.

Working alongside seasoned bakers and chefs, I felt firsthand the power of learning from experienced professionals. Their unique techniques, honed over years, were more than just skills; they were a legacy of craftsmanship passed down with each loaf of bread and sugar rose. This mentorship, an informal yet invaluable education, mirrors the mentor–mentee dynamics and the importance of hands-on learning I refer to throughout this book. The camaraderie and teamwork in that kitchen, where every role was integral to the final product, reflected the collaborative cultures I advocate for in the modern workplace. Just as each carefully shaped roll contributed to the warm, welcoming aroma of fresh bread at dawn, every individual in a team contributes to the collective success of an organization. My time at Gleneagles, with its blend of hard work, mentorship, and team cohesion, wasn't just about culinary artistry; it was a microcosm of the workforce principles I champion today: adaptability, skill development, and the transformative power of learning from those who have paved the path before us.

Adaptability in abundance: changing the dynamics of the workplace

Knowing how businesses must meet new exigencies, such as the Gleneagles Hotel transforming from a hotel to a hospital during WWII, I thought more about what it takes to adapt to a time of crisis. We witnessed this so recently during the pandemic.

World War II provides an interesting example of how the working dynamics of a nation can change almost overnight. The work ethic of civilians mobilized during the war was characterized by a strong sense of camaraderie and shared purpose. People from diverse backgrounds united with dedication, working tirelessly in factories and communities, driven by a collective commitment to support their nation's victory.

The first thing that stands out during such extremely challenging times is the power of teamwork. During wartime, not unlike the pandemic, people had to work together to achieve common goals. It should not take a war or a pandemic to revive this same spirit of collaboration, which can clearly benefit modern workplaces as well.

Flexibility and adaptability are the foundation of such transformations in business; being able to pivot quickly and respond to changing conditions was (and still is) essential for success.

But the most integral factor I found to be common from this era was that purpose drove commitment. Many workers during the war felt a strong sense of obligation to a higher purpose (certainly not pay or remuneration), whether it was defending their way of life, protecting their homeland, or supporting the war effort in other ways.

In the United States, the makeup of the workforce changed dramatically. With men off to war overseas, women stepped in and took over numerous jobs that now needed filling. This was an era in which far fewer women worked than we see today. It is estimated that between 5 and 6 million women entered the workforce between 1940 and 1945. As a result, the work environment shifted dramatically during the war years.

Rosie the Riveter

Rosie the Riveter was an allegorical cultural icon in the United States during the 1940s. She represented the many women who worked in factories and shipyards during World War II as riveters as well as in many other pivotal roles. Rosie was synonymous with female empowerment and American patriotism, representing a new chapter in the history of the American workforce.

Our journey through America's history begins in 1942, during World War II. At that time, the country faced an urgent need for workers in factories across the nation to support the war effort by building aircraft parts and other essential machinery. The answer to this labor shortage came from an overlooked demographic: women. Women across the country stepped up with courage and grace to take on jobs traditionally held by men while their husbands were away fighting the war overseas.

Although the true inspiration for, or identity of, Rosie the Riveter was debated for years, her story inspired a shift in America's workforce. Between 1940 and 1945, the female percentage of the US workforce increased from 27 percent to nearly 37 percent, and by 1945, nearly one out of every four married women worked outside the home, whereas others went to work right after leaving school.

In the twenty-first-century workplace, women professionals are increasingly taking on roles that were once considered off-limits due to gender biases. This shift has been accelerated by technological advances and groundbreaking initiatives designed to promote gender equality. From Silicon Valley tech giants to Wall Street powerhouses, women are now playing an integral role in the workforce. One such example is Dr. Janine Davis, a leading researcher at Google AI Lab who recently made history when she became the first African-American woman appointed to lead one of Google's research teams. Drawing inspiration from Rosie's legacy, Dr. Davis is determined to shatter glass ceilings and blaze new trails for young female professionals everywhere. She believes that technology can be used as a powerful tool in closing the gender gap, creating equal opportunities for all across industries and countries alike.

The story of Rosie the Riveter shows us just how much can be accomplished when individuals stand together against a common adversary, whether it's enemy troops, COVID-19, or discrimination, racism, and inequality.

The British Rosie the Riveter

British women also stepped up to the challenge and significantly contributed to the war effort. Many of them had never worked in a factory before, but they quickly adapted and learned new skills. Despite facing discrimination on occasion and being paid less than their male counterparts, they took pride in their work and were dedicated to supporting the war effort. During the London Blitz, a German bombing campaign against the United Kingdom, my grandmother, affectionately known as Nana Coombes, was a proud five-foot-one Scottish woman and a devoted admirer of the monarchy.

A shorter version of America's Rosie the Riveter, she was one of the many women who stepped up to fill the shortage of factory workers in England. During the day, she worked as a "clippie," selling tickets on London's double-decker buses. But at night, she worked at the Handley Page aircraft factory, helping assemble Halifax bombers. After the war, Nana Coombes emigrated to Australia as a "Ten Pound Pom," a nickname given to English immigrants based on the £10 processing fee to migrate. She worked in a shoe factory and served as a forelady, inspiring the Junior Girls (similar to America's Girl Scouts) to strive for excellence. She had a strong work ethic, took great pride in her work, showed gratitude, and was intent on giving back.

Professor, linguist, author, and spy

When exploring the camaraderie and shared spirit of those who willingly contributed to the war effort, I need to recognize and honor the resilience of individuals who endured forced labor during and after that period. My grandfather Milan was one of them.

My grandfather was a true multilingual talent. Fluent in four languages and proficient in several others, Milan worked for a news service agency, Agence Sud-Est, in Paris, covering Central Europe—a treacherous place to be when France fell under attack by the German army in 1940. Utilizing his linguistic abilities, he founded the radio station La Libre Tchécoslovaquie, operating until Vichy France took control. His escape from Paris echoed scenes from *Casablanca*, as he caught the last train out before the German occupation began. Like many Czechs, he fled to Martinique as a refugee. He applied his multilingual talents to recruiting for the Czechoslovak army in England under the guidance of Military Attaché General Oldřich Španiel, who coordinated the efforts from Washington, D.C. His unit was part of the Office of Strategic Services (OSS), which later evolved into the Central Intelligence Agency (CIA).

After the war, Milan worked as a press attaché at the Czechoslovak Embassy in Havana, Cuba. On returning to Czechoslovakia, like many Czechs, he was punished by the communist government for his wartime collaboration with the West and labeled "politically unreliable" by the Communist Party. By 1950, he was sent to a forced labor camp and put to work manufacturing ball bearings. Upon his release, he mysteriously met his end at a railway station not far from the camp, in the summer of 1957. His legacy as a professor, linguist, author, and spy endures as a poignant reminder to me of the multifaceted roles played by those caught in the currents of war and political change. Milan's story exemplifies the importance of resilience, multilingual and multicultural fluency, and the ability to make critical decisions under pressure. His journey, marked by courage and innovation in the face of adversity, serves as an inspiring blueprint for leaders who aim to steer their organizations through the challenges of the twenty-first century.

As Winston Churchill famously said, "We shall never surrender!" And if there's one thing we can learn from wartime work, it's the importance of resilience and persistence. As Churchill once joked, "Success is not final, failure is not fatal: it is the courage to continue that counts." I agree.

Unbreakable spirit

The journey to find meaning and purpose in work often leads us down unexpected paths and to encounters with unexpected characters. This brings me to Holdeen.

When I first met Holdeen, I was making a move from a hotel chef to the chef at a small restaurant. No, it was not one of my better moves. Holdeen was the outgoing chef, and his handover was filled with cynical criticism and insights about the restaurant, its shortcomings, and its owner. I would soon find out, within weeks, that what he had told me was actually very accurate. Yes, this was one of those jobs you drop from your resume.

Holdeen, however, was not someone I would drop from my life. His story was one of conquering demons, many of his own making, and doing whatever he had to do to succeed. As the story goes, nearly a decade earlier, on a hot summer day in Los Angeles, Holdeen sat perched on a wall overlooking a local Quick Mart, which is a combination of gas station and convenience store that could have justifiably had the sign "eat here, get gas" on the door.

Holdeen's unconventional approaches and unique perspectives
allowed him to breathe life into the mundane.

Holdeen, aged twenty at the time, was one of those people just hanging around without purpose. Behind him was a lemon tree, somewhat out of place but laden with fruit. For some reason, likely boredom, Holdeen had the idea to throw a lemon or two at passersby. In a moment of impulse, he began plucking lemons, one by one, and throwing them at people, watching intently for their reactions. Most just scuttled away; others made their displeasure known, some with universal hand gestures.

But one man, hit by a lemon, stopped in his tracks and pulled a handgun from his backpack. Holdeen, maybe driven by bravado or perhaps the naive courage of youth, jumped from the wall and ran towards the man. They wrestled and fell to the ground. And, not unlike the movies, amidst the tussle, a loud bang echoed across the lot. The gun had gone off.

Holdeen looked down, eyes wide in shock, his middle finger hanging by a thread. After the moment of stunned disbelief, he was whisked to a hospital where, despite the surgeon's best efforts, his finger could not be reattached.

Some people refuse to be forced into a mold, no matter how the world demands conformity. Holdeen, when I met him in his thirties, was still that square peg navigating a round hole. His unconventional approaches and unique perspectives allowed him to breathe life into the mundane, and that led him to a career as a chef. He could walk into a restaurant, whether it be a café or a Michelin star establishment, with no resume and no references, and proceed to cook a dish that would lead to him being instantly hired solely on his ability, no questions asked. He worked to afford travel and adventure. And when he had saved enough money to follow his latest dream or seek a new location, he would pick up and move on with only a few days' notice, generally to the extreme annoyance of his employers.

This led me to question the wisdom of handovers between new and old employees—passing the baton, as it were. Sometimes it becomes less about the technical work and more about personalities. And that's a recipe for disaster. Holdeen could cook. He was one of the best chefs I ever met. He introduced me to the homestyle flavors of Cajun and Creole cuisines, both native to Louisiana. Holdeen taught me how to cook blackened fish, hushpuppies, seafood gumbo, and jambalaya. He also unlocked for me some of the secrets of Catalonian cuisine, gained from his time in Spain, inspiring me to explore the food of this beautiful region further.

Holdeen gave me a book I treasure, *Catalan Cuisine: Europe's Last Great Culinary Secret*. It was written by Colman Andrews, who delved deep into the soul of this fiercely proud region of Spain. As you turn the pages, you can almost smell the smoky aroma of escalivada and hear the sizzle of seafood paella being cooked over an open flame. Well-used cookbooks like this, not the glossy coffee table formula books you often see, offer an invitation to explore a world brimming with passion, resilience, and flavors. There is not a single staged image in this book; it's just text and a few sketches. It's this kind of authenticity that is often missing in busy kitchens today, as well as in many businesses.

After several years of working on and off with Holdeen, I needed his help to launch a new restaurant venture. It seems that pubs, once located mostly in the country and suburbs, were becoming fashionable to a new younger demographic. So I jumped on the bandwagon and became part of the transformation of an old pub at the Grace Darling Hotel (built in 1852) in Melbourne, Australia.

Holdeen came in and helped me build a following. I had guided Holdeen out of a few tight spots, and despite his unreliability, he brought restaurant creativity in spades, which helped me to achieve a much-coveted One Chef's Hat in Australia, a sign of culinary excellence. This recognition is no small feat, as it signifies exceptional creativity and consistency in cuisine. Holdeen knew diddly about business and finance, but he had the gift of gab and talked his way into his own restaurant lease. I joined him sanding floors till the wee hours before the grand opening. The restaurant opened, and he was living his dream, albeit briefly, in a way only he could. Unfortunately, the restaurant tanked, so he left Australia and, sometime later, sent me an envelope with the key to a storage unit. I eventually opened it, and the first box was labeled "grandmother's head." *Okay*, I thought, *did this mean he was also a serial killer?* Thankfully, it just contained a bust of his grandmother. The rest of the unit had some old pots and pans and maybe a hundred cookbooks. I still have a few, and others I have given to up-and-coming chefs as a point of inspiration.

Holdeen's past didn't matter to me; his zest for his chosen career and his creativity serve as a message to us all: to take some risks and embrace the unconventional. In the end, my crazy mate Holdeen found his final peace not in the chaos of a kitchen or the grind of the city but in the United States, in the untamed wilderness of Washington state, a place where he so often sought solace. As with many of life's turns, he found new love, yet in a tragic twist of fate, nature claimed him in the very landscape that inspired him.

Holdeen's journey illustrates the profound impact of embracing our unique talents and creating a fulfilling career path. His story is a testament to the extraordinary potential that lies within each of us: we must simply dare to embrace our unique talents and chart our own unconventional paths. As we remember Holdeen's unbreakable spirit, let us draw inspiration and courage to pursue our passions, innovate, and craft a career that not only drives success but also resonates with our deepest values and aspirations. Also remember that often the most unconventional routes lead to the most fulfilling destinations.

They remind us that the ingredients for success aren't always found in the conventional recipe books of career planning guides. It's often the mavericks, the outliers, who bring a unique flavor to the table, spicing up the traditional with a dash of the unexpected.

Stories of people like Holdeen not only inspire us but also challenge us to rethink our approach to work, creativity, and success. In doing so, we foster a culture of innovation and inclusivity, in which different talents can flourish and contribute to a collective success that's as diverse as it is dynamic.

Meeting Her Royal Highness

I conclude this section by shifting to a very different chapter in my life, one filled with some levity among lessons learned about people of different backgrounds and social classes.

For years, I had wanted to visit the royal residence of Balmoral Castle, located on the bank of the River Dee, which winds through the Scottish countryside toward the North Sea.

On a rare day off, I decided to put on my comfortable walking shoes and visit the Balmoral estate, which covers more than 50,000 acres of forests, farmland, and moorland with stunning landscapes and abundant wildlife. Though it's not strongly advertised, when the royal family is not in residence, they often open parts of the estate for visitors to enjoy. Thanks to an inside contact from my culinary adventures, I was able to access a more private side of Balmoral. As I stood at the gates of Balmoral, a quarter-Scottish blood running through me, the connection to my ancestral roots felt more tangible than ever.

Following a lengthy security check, I found myself inside the grounds of Balmoral Castle. And it just so happened to be the estate staff's annual fancy dress evening, which included a spectrum of costumes, many inspired by the royal vegetable patch. I knew a few of the staff members, and scored a last-minute invitation to the event. Unbeknownst to me, the queen was in attendance at this fancy affair and was tasked with judging the best-dressed awards. She walked through the room, and her gaze shifted from the array of staffers dressed as vegetables to me, out of place, devoid of a carrot or turnip costume. I'm sure that upon her noticing me, I probably struck a deer-in-headlights pose. And then, with gracious curiosity, she started walking in my direction, and as she passed by, she asked softly, "Where do you work?" Surprised, I responded, "Gleneagles, ma'am."

She stopped walking, paused, and had a look of bemusement as she continued. "Oh, Gleneagles," she echoed, probably wondering how someone from Gleneagles Hotel was at her Balmoral staff party.

She continued on her way, and I resumed my deer-caught-in-headlights pose, expecting to be led out the door in handcuffs, perhaps by a security guard dressed as a zucchini. But, after a few moments, I looked around and saw nobody approaching. I was not yet asked to leave or carried away, so I decided I should mingle, which I did. In a series of conversations with Balmoral's royal chef, I discovered an unexpected fondness for the *Australian Women's Weekly* cookbooks, recipe books known for their comforting and simple dishes that capture the essence of home-cooked meals. They feature classic Australian comfort foods like hearty stews and lamingtons. The chef confided that Her Royal Highness had a penchant for straightforward recipes. "She prefers it plain," he whispered, affirming the queen's like for simple dishes and low-key dinners in front of the TV. After all, Balmoral was her holiday house.

Being on the Balmoral grounds or in the general area surrounding the castle, you must remember to keep your eyes peeled. A cloud of dust, and you might catch a glimpse of the queen roaring past in the driver's seat of her Land Rover. Her skills behind the wheel were no mere show; she had trained as a driver and mechanic and worked in the motor pool during the war, where she learned to maintain and repair vehicles. At dusk, the family secured the inner sanctum, with some security outside the gates consisting of modern London Bobbies (i.e., police officers), dressed informally in deerstalker hats to blend in with the Highlands vibe.

In a world driven by virtual connections, witnessing the joy of people actually donning costumes and enjoying nature was a breath of fresh air, reminiscent of the simple pleasures that come from setting aside technology to savor a board game with family. I was also aware that in a world of extreme security, I was able to chat for a moment with Her Majesty without security turning it into an international incident.

Buckingham Palace

More recently, I received an invite to Buckingham Palace. Really. This was because of my association with Lord Kenneth Baker, the chairman of the Edge Foundation, dedicated to teaching the next generation the skills necessary to meet ever-changing global, digital, and economic demands. He liked my work on apprenticeships enough to invite me to speak at some of the foundation's events. We hit it off and became acquaintances. Lord Baker was the education secretary under Margaret Thatcher, which is pretty cool. So he arranged for me to get an invite to the palace. I was even invited to have tea with him at the House of Lords!

Plus, I got to meet the Duke of York.

As I arrived at the enormous black iron palace gates, I entered through high security. No doubt, palace security ramped up ever since Michael Fagan, a somewhat "ordinary" member of society, decided one night that he needed to chat with the queen, immediately. He scaled the palace walls, climbed up a drainpipe, and entered the queen's bedroom, where she awoke to find him sitting on the end of her bed. They chatted until security eventually arrived. Fagan was not charged with trespassing but with stealing a bottle of wine, a crime for which he was later acquitted. Imagine how frightening that was for the queen, or for anyone, to be woken up by a stranger sitting on the end of their bed in the middle of the night. Had Fagan attempted a similar intrusion in the United States, he would likely have encountered someone who would invoke the equivalent of the British Castle Doctrine, a legal principle that permits the use of deadly force to protect oneself within their own home if they believe their life is in danger.

Once through the front gates, I walked across the large gravel forecourt where the famous changing of the guard takes place. I was then greeted by a gentleman holding a silver tray requesting politely, "Your telecommunications device, sir." Clearly this tradition does not extend very far back. You place your cell phone on the tray, and he slips it into a small velvet drawstring bag and, in exchange, hands you a quaint little wooden numbered token. Now it was time for tea. At the top of the large staircase, I was met with the aroma of freshly brewed tea—not a tea bag in sight. This is loose tea leaves left to steep in a teapot and poured through a strainer into a bone china teacup, with milk and sugar added to your liking. A piece of Scottish shortbread, and you are all set.

The students did a presentation as we observed. But a short conversation with the prince between presentations left me a little perplexed. I commented, "It's fantastic to watch all these young people. They have their lives ahead of them; they can do anything they want to do and be anything they want to be." Although that is true for most of us, apparently the prince had a different view. "Not for me," he replied with a wry smile that bore an undercurrent of disappointment. I had not thought about it, but as "the prince," he does not have a whole lot of choices as to what occupation he might take. From the moment of his birth, everything is preordained.

Reflecting on these royal adventures, I am reminded that true fulfillment isn't measured by extravagance or luxury; it's found in the lessons we learn, the empathy we gain, and the compassion we extend to others, especially those facing hardship. Do titles and extravagance equate to happiness? That's for each to determine. What I realized from my brief brushes with royalty was that although they live very different and more extravagant lifestyles than most, they, like the rest of us, are people with their own tastes, likes, dislikes, challenges, and secrets. Who knew that Her Royal Highness liked rather plain food or the prince might secretly desire another field of employment? All in all, my morning tea at the palace is an experience I will never forget.

CHAPTER 8

Happy and Motivated Employees

———

HAPPY AND MOTIVATED EMPLOYEES ARE PARAMOUNT TO any successful company. In 1961, as urban legend would have it that on his tour of NASA headquarters, President John F. Kennedy encountered a janitor mopping the floors. When President Kennedy asked the man why he was working so late, the janitor responded, "Mr. President, I'm helping put a man on the moon." This story illustrates the motivation that can drive a team to success.

Recognizing the pivotal role of employee motivation in organizational success is essential. The right strategies in purchasing and marketing can fuel a company's expansion, but an inspired workforce is the real powerhouse. Let's turn to a historical example for inspiration. During World War II, Winston Churchill, known for his charismatic leadership and resolve, provided a standout example of motivation under pressure. Amid the harrowing London Blitz, Churchill opted to witness the bombing firsthand from a rooftop. When questioned about this daring act, his response was simple yet profound: "I want to see the war." This wasn't mere recklessness; it was a bold testament to his commitment to lead and inspire amidst crisis. Churchill's actions justly characterize his leadership: an unyielding spirit in the face of adversity that motivated an entire nation.

So what ignites employee motivation? It's that inner drive propelling employees to excel, to contribute wholeheartedly, and to align their success with the company's vision. It's something within them that makes the work more worthwhile. As children, our parents let us watch TV or play outside once we finished our homework. These were simply motivational ways to get a child to complete a task. As one gets older, motivation comes in many and more complex shapes and forms. Often, very successful people are motivated by the financial hardships they saw in their families growing up. They are motivated to achieve more and provide a better life for their families.

In business, employees are often motivated by the idea that their work impacts others in a positive manner. The CEO of a California-based medical supplies company often explained that she was proud of her team because they were all especially motivated to create the absolute best products possible, knowing they would be used in operating rooms to save lives. So let's not overlook the importance of employee motivation. Instead, we should invest in strategies that inspire and empower our employees to do their best work and be their best selves.

In 1943, Abraham Maslow proposed a theory of human motivation that provides a framework for understanding what motivates people. He noted that human beings have a hierarchy of needs that must be satisfied in a particular order.

Here are the five needs in Maslow's hierarchy and how they can be addressed in a modern workplace:

- **Physiological needs (hunger and thirst):** Companies can provide adequate breaks and rest periods, as well as access to healthy food and drinks in the workplace.

- **Safety needs (security and stability):** Occupational health and safety measures should be implemented, and financial security can be guaranteed by offering employees appropriate wages, sick pay, and company pensions. Order and stability can be created through transparent career paths, permanent employment contracts, and disclosure of the strategic development of the organization.

- **Social needs (camaraderie and belonging):** Companies can encourage teamwork to provide opportunities for social interaction and offer employee engagement programs.

- Esteem needs (self-esteem and respect from others): Companies can recognize and reward good performance, offer opportunities for career advancement, and provide positive feedback and constructive criticism.

- **Self-actualization needs (personal development and fulfillment):** Managers can offer continuing education and training courses, promote individual strengths, provide meaningful tasks, transfer autonomy, offer opportunities to engage in creativity and innovation, and strengthen the sense of purpose at work.

Maslow's hierarchy of needs gives us a structure to understand the complexity of employee motivation and help companies derive concrete measures for improving employee satisfaction.

The janitor that JFK encountered was just a small part of a much larger story unfolding at NASA, but he had an important role to play. This story emphasizes the point that no matter how large or small your role, everyone contributes to the larger story of the business or organization. When everyone on a team embraces this attitude and belief system, incredible things can happen.

Creating a pleasant workplace culture is crucial for any company. In fact, research from Harvard shows that happy employees can increase sales by up to 37% compared with their unhappy colleagues.[1] That's a huge boost to productivity and revenue. Many more studies have been done with similar results.

We've learned over the years that benefits of happy employees go beyond just the bottom line. According to research by the University of Oxford, happy employees are more resilient, less likely to be absent because of illness or burnout, and less likely to leave their jobs. This translates to better retention rates, significant cost savings for companies, and a stronger sense of loyalty and commitment from employees.[2]

So how can companies keep their employees happy (apart from the obvious pay hikes)? Let's summarize.

- **Flexibility is vital:** Offering flexible working hours and locations gives employees the creative freedom they need to do their best work. Whether it's working from home, taking a sabbatical, or compressing the workweek, flexible arrangements allow employees to find the work and life balance that works for them.

- **Positive vibes:** By promoting creative freedom, focusing on employee strengths, and rewarding individual success, companies can foster an environment where employees feel valued and motivated to do their best. Equally important is what leaders shouldn't do. Positives become negatives when leaders blame employees, shame employees, or create unnecessary stress through micromanaging or cutting off open lines of communication. It also helps not to gossip and to make as few assumptions about your employees or your team as possible.

- **Feedback is essential:** Managers should offer constructive feedback that helps employees grow while also recognizing their strengths and successes. But it's not just about managers; employees should also be encouraged to offer feedback to their superiors. Open communication helps avoid frustration and burnout while also motivating employees to perform their best. Finally, feedback should always focus on the task or work at hand, not the person.

- **Work–life balance matters:** Companies that prioritize work–life balance and meaningful work are more likely to keep employees engaged and committed.

When life gives you lemons … drink gin! ☺

One of the oldest and most revered food stores in the world is Fortnum & Mason in London, which is known for its exquisite selection of foods and goods. Fortnum's top floor houses something quite unique: a microdistillery. This distillery is a part of a booming boutique gin movement, capturing the essence of craft and tradition.

Just as the distillation of gin involves refining and perfecting, my journey to becoming a chef, which would eventually lead me to London, was a process of evaluating and honing my skills and aspirations. This journey was marked by many ups and downs. Yet each step played a vital part in shaping my future.

As I approached the end of high school, I knew that I wanted to become a chef, and my dad and I worked tirelessly together to find me an apprenticeship. After many applications and interviews—including one intriguing info session—I was finally starting on this new path.

My first interview at the Southern Cross Hotel, however, didn't quite go as planned. I confidently strode into a grand ballroom, only to be taken aback by its intimidating opulence. To make matters worse, I accidentally entered through the main entrance reserved for guests, not the back entrance for prospective candidates or hotel employees. It felt like an omen.

Although the interviewers were unimpressed with my limited work history, I didn't let their advice about starting "at the bottom" discourage me.

Continuing my search, I applied and interviewed for an apprenticeship at the iconic Windsor Hotel. The entire experience was nerve-wracking, from navigating past the top-hatted doorman, making sure to enter through the service entrance this time, to filling out the arduous packet of paperwork. But when I finally made it to the personnel officer's desk, I felt hopeful and excited.

During the interview, I was asked to share a difficult situation from the workplace. I recalled an incident from my after-school job at a grocery store, where the manager would dip into multiple bottles of detergent from the shop's shelves to mop the store floor. When he saw me gape in surprise, he simply assured me, "Don't worry, customers won't know." This incident made me ponder how far honesty can be stretched. In the end, I left the interview feeling confident about landing the apprenticeship opportunity.

Despite my enthusiasm and effort, two letters soon arrived informing me that I had not been selected. I now see those moments of rejection not just as setbacks but as the universe guiding me towards my true path. I would go on to learn that every setback also creates an opportunity for a comeback. Rejection is also a source of motivation.

Similarly, someone who embodies this spirit of embracing life's challenges is my young friend Joyce. Despite living with cerebral palsy, Joyce is a determined young person. When we first met, she told me about a local community center that takes her out for trips into the community. About these community excursions, Joyce explained that "they were fun for a season, but honestly, I was longing for something more." With support from Kiki, her foster mother, Joyce aspired to have a fulfilling career, not just a job. I connected her with a wonderful mentor named Jordan from the Ready, Willing & Able program (in collaboration with the California Department of Rehabilitation). This proved to be a turning point. Jordan and Joyce set a plan, got her some skills preemployment training, and Joyce has since gained a full-time job in the medical field as a biller and coder. Her journey is a testament to the power of resilience and the importance of aiming high, no matter the obstacles. She turned her setbacks into a story of success and continues to inspire those around her. When last we spoke, she told me about having "a sense of purpose being in a career helping people. It's so rewarding." It's a reminder that when life throws challenges our way, there's always a way to create a positive and empowering future.

Cooking, connecting, and celebrating

As I reflected on the power of community and shared experiences, a recent adventure in Madrid brought these principles to life in the most delightful way. Let me share the story of "Cooking, Connecting, and Celebrating," a journey that not only tantalized our taste buds but also strengthened our bonds as individuals and as a family.

Sweat dotted my brow as I stood around a massive paella pan with its rich contents bubbling away. It was one of six in the room. Along with my wife, Prue, and our two teenagers, James and Alexandra, we were joined by twenty strangers from the United States, Singapore, and across Europe who gathered to meet, cook, chat, dance, and eat in an old stone building in Madrid built in the early 1900s. During the pandemic, Nicaraguan chef Erick Belli, along with his business partner, Alex Villar, took on the abandoned shell and transformed it into the home of The Cooking Clubhouse.

Chef Belli explained his motivation: "I've been a chef in big hotels in Miami, New York, Berne, and the Canary Islands. But while serving food feeds the body, it can also feed the soul. My target has always been that."

The author and his children, Alexandra and James,
at The Cooking Clubhouse in Madrid, Spain.

What's unique about The Cooking Clubhouse is that it makes paying guests do their own cooking. As a chef, I expected to dust off my food preparation skills for this experience. But when my family and I arrived, all the ingredients had been precisely cut, prepared, and laid out for us, as they were identically for each participant. Belli says, "We do all the hard work so that you can follow the recipes, and I'll guide you." On arrival, adults are handed a glass of Cava, a sparkling Spanish wine, and the work begins on preparing our five-course meal, including tapas. It was as much about cooking as it was about engaging with others—a celebration of food in life, very motivational, and something completely different. Belli says sometimes his guests cry, and that's not just due to the onions. "They haven't had this human connection for a long time. They remember what it's like to interact with people outside of their everyday experiences. It grounds them a bit."

Our session was one of three Belli and his team of eight held each day. The roster is a good fit but not demanding. "The gastro world has a vicious cycle of employees working too many hours," Belli says. "It's too demanding and stressful. Our jobs are where we spend most of our day. If you don't feel happy, comfortable, or appreciated, what's the point of going to that place?" He raises a good point.

This immersive experience at The Cooking Clubhouse embodies the essence of what it means to foster a kindness movement in the workplace. The story of Erick Belli and his unique culinary venture underscores the power of creating spaces where people can come together, learn, share, and grow. Businesses can benefit from ideas like The Cooking Clubhouse. In fact, they can set one up once every few months for their employees. Pro tip: get a list of what attendees can and cannot eat.

How to find meaning and purpose in your work

When employees are personally invested in what a company does or stands for, they have a greater focus and are more committed and dedicated to their positions. In some cases, the initiatives, and even the company's products or services, have a significant impact on some part of society and make the world a drop better for everyone, as well as for the planet. For example, a company may be involved in healthier product solutions that do not pollute our environment. Think Patagonia, which makes wetsuits from natural rubber and turns plastic bottles into parkas. Then there's IKEA. Fifty percent of the wood in its furniture comes from sustainable foresters and all of its cotton from farms that meet the standards set by the Better Cotton Initiative, such as using less water, energy, or pesticides. Many companies, from banks and insurance companies to small businesses, also support one or many sustainable goals that align employees to the business at a personal level. Read online about companies you would like to work for, and research what sustainable initiatives they support, but keep a critical eye. Remember what I said earlier about greenwashing.

A journey to discover what matters most

What does it all mean? This question has perplexed philosophers and thinkers throughout history. I am fortunate to be the custodian of a painting I walk past nearly every day that reminds me of this. It raises questions about the meaning of life through the lens of artist Corinna Heumann, who is driven by a love for beauty, truth, and the idea that art can connect people on a deeper level.

She believes that art is the meaningful communication of immaterial values and that everything that makes up a person and gives life meaning can be expressed through art. As we go through our daily lives, it's easy to get caught up in our routines and forget to take a step back and think about what we're trying to achieve.

Was Soll Das Bedeuten, **painting by Corinna Heumann**

Today, countless ideas and initiatives are vying for our attention, which can lead to confusion and the feeling of being overwhelmed.

Every time I look at it, the painting reminds me to take a step back and reflect on what gives my life meaning and purpose. Often, I feel like there's simply not enough time in the day to focus on what's truly important. I've talked with many other people who have this same conundrum. So how can we cut through the noise and work out what's worth our time and attention? Stop for a moment and consider what occupies your time and how it aligns with what matters most to you.

Here's a simple exercise you might try. Grab a piece of paper, or go to a drawing app on your smartphone, and draw a line down the middle, labeling one side "pluses" and the other "minuses." What are the things that are important for you to do? This might be spending time with your family, focusing on doing well at your job, learning, exercising, dancing, singing, painting, volunteering, traveling, or anything that makes you feel good about yourself. List these on the "pluses" side. What are things that take up additional time but do not benefit you personally or financially? Examples of "minuses" might include mindlessly scrolling through social media, attending unnecessary meetings that don't contribute to your goals, engaging in gossip or negative conversations, overcommitting to social obligations that leave you drained, or even persisting with hobbies that no longer bring you joy. Jot down everything that is happening in your current life in one column or the other. Then step back and look at what falls in each category. This will give you a clear picture of what's working well and what's not.

Striving to be the best: an insider's look at the precision and excellence of Porsche

Many companies strive for excellence, but while such companies may enjoy great success, reaching a level of brilliance is a greater challenge. Meet Niven Tsing, whose story stands out as a testament to the power of passion and perseverance. With a robust academic background in science and marketing, Niven seemed predestined for a straight shot up the corporate ladder. Yet beneath this structured exterior simmered his true calling: a profound affinity for classic cars. He loved Porsche models especially. This steered Niven down a more unconventional career path (no pun intended). He took a leap—threw in his old career and entered the world of automotive technology. His interest and dedication soon led to an apprenticeship at a factory-owned Porsche store, a significant stride in his quest to join this industry.

Niven's initial time at Porsche as a first-year apprentice laid the foundation of his journey. He grasped the importance of starting from the basics, recognizing that mastery in any field begins with a thorough understanding of its fundamentals. The learning curve required more than just understanding technology and mechanical intricacies; it involved immersing himself in the company's ethos and in a culture steeped in history and innovation.

Porsche, established in 1931 by Ferdinand Porsche in Stuttgart, Germany, initially focused on motor vehicle development and consulting rather than manufacturing cars. Ferdinand Porsche was already a notable figure in the automotive world, having worked on electric vehicles, including the Lohner-Porsche back in 1900, one of the earliest electric cars. (Yes, there were electric cars long before Elon Musk came around.) A pivotal assignment for Ferdinand Porsche was designing the Volkswagen Beetle in the 1930s, a car that would become one of history's most iconic and bestselling vehicles.

For Niven, a significant turning point came when his dedication and hard work were recognized with a prestigious award from his community college. This accolade led him to a scholarship and Porsche's headquarters in Germany, where he gained invaluable insights into the brand's storied past and meticulous craftsmanship, and where he came to appreciate even more the genesis of the cars he worked on.

Niven's narrative is about more than a career transition. In a world where traditional career paths are increasingly replaced by more dynamic pursuits, Niven's journey shines as an inspiration for those yearning to blend their career with their passion.

Niven's story even inspired me to embark on my own Porsche adventure. It was a tough job, but in the name of research for this book, I found myself in Stuttgart, Germany.

Arriving at Porsche Museum in Stuttgart, you can't help but notice the striking sculpture of three Porsche 911s, each representing a different era, that dominates the central roundabout. That's right, the impressive eighty-plus-foot sculpture features three real Porsche cars—a brand new 911 and a couple of classics restored to showroom condition.

The museum building is futuristic, with clean, sleek lines, resting on three giant V-shaped columns, giving the appearance that the building is floating. With street parking not an option, as that would ruin the aesthetic of this architectural masterpiece, I followed the signs to the underground *parkplatz*. The carpark was also like a museum, with some seriously cool cars.

Dragging my children away from the fancy rides in the carpark, we caught the lift into the main building, and after a quick pit stop at the Porche café, we met our guide and entered the museum. Up a very long escalator, you see a showcase of both historic and contemporary Porsche models as far as the eye can see.

Our guide led us through many interesting exhibits. One that stood out was to the Porsche 919 Hybrid; its sleek design and World Endurance Championship pedigree captivated us. Inviting children into the museum was a great move; the folks at Porsche clearly like to educate in hopes of gleaning the next generation of Porsche enthusiasts. James and Alex were given white cloth gloves, and after making sure they had no buckles or any metal that could scratch a car, they were allowed to step over the rope and engage with a few exhibits, including sitting in some of these magnificent vehicles and holding the steering wheel of this classic 919 Hybrid Evo. What's an Evo, you ask? As hybrids go, this was a fast unit—some 1160 horsepower, and it lapped the famous Nürburgring motorsports complex in five minutes and nineteen seconds, setting a new record. The car also bore the numerous names of mechanics, engineers, designers, and various professionals involved in designing and building the Evo—a lovely symbol of the

collective effort and expertise integral to the 919 Hybrid's achievements. This recognition of teamwork and the often-overlooked heroes
behind these machines deeply resonated with me. How cool is that?
Good one, Porsche.

Ushered out of the museum by tour guides tapping their watches,
we walked across the plaza with a small group, noting the disjointed
layout of the 911 factory. It was sprawling across a busy road between
two enormous factory buildings. Apparently, Ferdinand Porsche never
envisioned the monumental expansion of Porsche and its indelible
link to Stuttgart. Today, Porsche wants to maintain the tradition and
remain at the birthplace of this iconic car—but with that comes serious
space constraints.

Upstairs in the Porsche factory, we were immediately struck by the
symphony of precision and human craftsmanship. Here, in this 188-
acre facility teeming with 3,000 employees, every two-door Porsche
model, including the entire 911 range, is meticulously crafted on a
single production line. This series production approach, blending
standardization with customization, is a masterstroke in manufacturing efficiency.

One notable aspect is the removal of vehicle doors as they move
down the production line. This practice, common in the industry yet
executed with an extra layer of precision here, provides workers with
enhanced access to the vehicle interiors, facilitating an efficient and
precise assembly process. The Porsche workforce is the epitome of
expertise and dedication. People are dressed like the vehicles: professional, with nothing out of place. Each employee's high level of formal
training was evident in the meticulous attention to detail and the seam-
less execution of each task. It's this human element, the skilled hands
that were crafting these cars, while using technology.

The strategic placement of robots and mechanical arms was also impressive. These machines, used for particular tasks such as fitting dashboards, are not just tools but partners in production. They reduce the physical strain on workers, moving large heavy objects with precision and ease.

Perhaps the most striking feature of the facility was its vertical, multifloor design. Equipped with vast car elevators and conveyors suspended over the production line, the design is a brilliant solution to the problem of limited space.

As we left the factory, the impression was clear: the Porsche factory in Stuttgart is a place where automotive dreams are forged into reality and where some seriously organized work gets accomplished daily. This is a place where legacy meets the cutting edge of automotive technology and where the skill of a dedicated workforce blends with innovative manufacturing techniques. This creates not just cars but works of art on wheels that everyone associated with the company can be proud of. This is also the right recipe to attract skilled workers.

CHAPTER 9

Underrepresented
Represents Opportunity

———

EVERYONE DESERVES TO BE SEEN, RESPECTED, AND VAL-
ued in the workplace. We have made great strides in building a diverse
workforce, but there's still much more work to do. Women and people
of color still face barriers for higher-paying positions and leadership
roles. Underrepresented populations, such as the LGBTQ+ community and those from low-income backgrounds, bring untapped
potential when given a chance through fair and equal access. Recent
immigrants as well as refugees, not to mention older individuals, also
need to be fairly represented. Diversity has been proven time and again
to enhance innovation, which leads to greater productivity amongst all
employees—this is why inclusion matters now more than ever before.

Diversity is especially necessary in the hospitality industry, with
which I am well acquainted. At a recent stay at a Hilton Hotel, something different caught my eye. In the reception area, I noticed a flyer
about their diversity and inclusion program. Usually, I think this is just
another corporate statement, but I was curious. So I asked the receptionist at the desk about it. She explained that it wasn't just a PR thing,

adding that Hilton focuses on making everyone feel welcome, be it employees or guests. They're living it every day, not just checking a box.

She went on to tell me about the initiatives they have, such as focusing on getting more women into leadership roles around the hotel and ensuring there's no pay gap. And this receptionist's speech wasn't rehearsed; it was genuine. This woman was honestly proud to be part of a company that's actively working towards making a difference.

It was just a brief conversation, but it stuck with me. It's impressive when a company's values are so ingrained that every employee, from the receptionist to top management, not only knows about it but believes in it. This makes you want to keep coming back.

See the ability, not the disability

People with disabilities have historically been overlooked and underrepresented in the workforce. Despite a shortage of skilled workers in the United States, only 22.5 percent of people with disabilities are employed. The unemployment rate for people with disabilities is more than double that of those without disabilities. Companies can benefit from including people with disabilities in the workplace, and they can do that by providing training and support to employees and making inclusion a top priority. Programs highlighting the importance of inclusion and providing ongoing support to employees with disabilities can effectively create a more inclusive workplace. Companies that follow this approach will find skilled and eager workers ready to build careers.

Meet Derrick. His story showcases how inclusive workforce support systems can build careers. Derrick, who uses a wheelchair, started as a mature-age apprentice. He later became a dispensing optician.

When I asked him about his work, he said, "I never imagined that I could do this work. It's been amazing. At the start, I struggled, too, but there's a net around me to help me grow into the role. It's a powerful program which changes lives."

Another inspirational person I know is Jazmin. She is a prime example of resilience and empowerment. Jazmin discovered a new world of opportunities in the healthcare sector, an area in which she had no prior experience. Despite the challenges posed by her dyslexia, she excelled in her apprenticeship, gaining skills and confidence. Jazmin reflected on her experience, saying, "This experience has been something that taught me a new world. I came into this apprenticeship with no medical knowledge, and now I'm leading study groups and achieving straight-*A* grades. It's so rewarding." Her journey underscores the potential and dedication individuals with disabilities bring to the workplace when given the opportunities.

Learning from the stories of Derrick and Jazmin and my conversations with them, here are some actionable steps for creating a more inclusive work environment for people with disabilities:

- **Improve accessibility:** Make sure people with disabilities have the same access as nondisabled people throughout your location(s) of business, including offices, stores, factories, etc. Also check that your website, job postings, and other digital materials meet accessibility standards. You can use the World Wide Web Consortium's Web Content Accessibility Guidelines.

- **Rethink recruitment:** Advertise roles in a way that indicates accessibility and is welcoming to people with disabilities.

Ensure that technology platforms used in recruitment are accessible, and consider partnering with local organizations to reach and attract a wider pool of candidates.

- **Onboard effectively:** Once you've hired someone with a disability, ensure that your onboarding process considers their needs. You may offer mentoring, opportunities for open communication, and access to support programs. Document your process, and review it regularly to ensure it's truly inclusive.

In my work, I advocate for a unique approach to disability employment. It's not about urging employers to hire individuals solely because of their disability or to create special roles for them. Instead, it's about identifying the precise skills that each role requires. With this understanding, I then work with candidates who have disabilities, focusing on the roles or careers they are interested in. The goal is to bridge any gaps—be it in skills, experience, or other areas—to facilitate these candidates' successful entry into the workplace.

Here's how it looks from a company's perspective. During my visit to the UPS Transitional Learning Center in Louisville, Kentucky, I encountered a unique and highly effective training program. I witnessed firsthand how UPS has committed itself to better serve and support the community, particularly individuals with disabilities. This program, developed in partnership with a local nonprofit, is dedicated to providing essential preemployment training, covering everything from job duties and safety protocols to mastering interpersonal skills.

What truly sets this program apart is the unique environment it provides participants to practice on-the-job skills without the pressure of being on the job. UPS has ingeniously designed a simulated production line within its training facility. This simulation allows participants to gain real-time experience in a controlled environment, gradually building their confidence and skills. This thoughtful design ensures that participants are well prepared and comfortable before they transition into mainstream orientation and then operations.

A second chance

Take a walk with me through the bustling streets of Melbourne, Australia, during the stormy 1940s—a time overshadowed by global conflict. Amid this chaos, Café Petrushka stood tall, radiating warmth and love. This intimate establishment on Little Collins Street was the brainchild of Jessica Sumner, a woman who expressed her love through the language of food.

Born and raised in Manchester, England, Jessica had no formal culinary training. Yet her natural understanding of flavors, textures, and the art of blending ingredients into perfect symphonies of taste compensated for her lack of education.

At Café Petrushka, it was not about fancy presentations or gourmet delicacies. Instead, it was a haven of heartwarming, home-cooked meals that spoke volumes about love, care, and passion. Each plate reflected Jessica's journey. The café quickly became a magnet, attracting a diverse clientele. Tables buzzed with conversations about topics ranging from art and philosophy to world affairs and everyday life. This distinctive setting broke down barriers, allowing a judge to share a laugh with a dockworker or an artist to discuss color palettes with a priest. All this accompanied by Jessica's culinary creations gave you the perfect melting pot atmosphere.

However, beyond the conversations and community, Jessica's philosophy shone through: love and care are best expressed through food.

The lingering aroma of simmering stews and aromatic coffee brought anyone and everyone the feeling of being cherished and cared for.

Though the café was undeniably successful, Jessica's heart yearned for more, leading her to the Brotherhood of St. Laurence, a monumental nonprofit institution dedicated to social justice. There she found purpose alongside Father Gerard Tucker, a beacon of hope for the oppressed. Their missions aligned, united by a shared dream of lifting society's less fortunate and relieving them of their burdens.

The Brotherhood was more than just a charity; it was a network of philanthropic individuals woven together with triumphs, adversities overcome, and boundless compassion. Jessica's culinary skills and intrinsic drive to serve converged within its walls. Her meals became more than sustenance; they were stories, love, and memories plated up. Through her food, she offered hope and comfort to those seeking refuge from life's storms.

It was through the Brotherhood that Jessica first met Kim, a twenty-two-year-old Czech immigrant whose troubled past included being incarcerated. This weighed heavily on him. Throwing Kim a lifeline in the form of a job driving a truck for the Brotherhood, Jessica gave him more than just employment; she offered him redemption and a second chance at life.

As Kim delivered meals and supplies—the many miles driven in his truck representing his journey from past mistakes to brighter prospects—Jessica's compassionate presence guided him towards a renewed sense of purpose. The job transformed Kim's life, inspiring him to pursue social work and eventually become a respected psychologist, following in Jessica's footsteps as a social worker.

The Brotherhood of St. Laurence and Kim's transformative journey were all intertwined, woven together by Jessica's unwavering spirit of service and compassion. She was a social worker for a quarter of a century until tragedy struck with the devastating loss of both her parents in a house fire. This untimely twist of fate thrust Jessica into a profound state of isolation and solitude.

Beneath her loving, generous front, Jessica concealed painful scars. Though she was seen as a symbol of hope to many, she bore her burdens—perhaps the haunting memories of lost love, the remorse for unexplored opportunities, or simply the overwhelming responsibility of being a pillar of support for so many. Although the world knew her as Jessica the caregiver, only a select few glimpsed the vulnerabilities she kept hidden within.

Jessica Sumner sought refuge from the outside world in a house hidden behind weathered newspapers and tall fences. She intentionally chose solitude as a means of finding comfort and peace. She embraced a simple lifestyle, relying on the soft glow of candles and lanterns for light and layering her clothing for warmth. The accumulation of garbage served as a reminder of her solitary existence, and her meals consisted mainly of canned food, a far cry from the elaborate culinary delights she once created and enjoyed.

Despite her age, Jessica refused outside help, once climbing onto the roof with a linen cloth and a can of tar to patch a hole. Her resourcefulness was a desperate attempt to keep the outside world at bay.

Living in isolation, Jessica disconnected herself from the hustle and bustle of the modern world. Her property became overgrown with wild plants covering the windows and transforming the once beautiful garden into a dense wilderness. There was no electricity, gas, or heating, but this was the life she willingly chose.

A friendship had formed with Kim, now a chief executive of a membership organization of general practitioners at a leading hospital.

Grateful for the second chance Jessica provided her husband during his challenging transition from incarceration, Kim's wife, Roberta, would often leave care packages for Jessica, lowering them on a rope over her back fence. Roberta would sometimes take their teenage son along on her missions. He was young and curious, often wondering about the woman living behind the windows covered in newspapers. The mystery of her reclusive lifestyle intrigued him.

Boxing Day (a holiday in England during which you traditionally give boxes of gifts or money to those in need) was significant in Jessica's heart. Following Christmas, she would emerge from her secluded home to visit Kim and his family at their residence. Their son eagerly awaited these visits, as they were an opportunity to hear Jessica's captivating stories. These tales of Jessica's vibrant past unfolded over time, each teaching valuable lessons and painting vivid pictures in the young boy's mind. Jessica Sumner's life transitioned from a distant story to a personal and impactful narrative, shaping the boy's perceptions and beliefs.

As time passed, the son grew into a young man, and he began to understand the contrasting aspects of Jessica's life—the tragedy that led to her isolation, the boundless love she possessed, and the reason for his parents' connection with her.

Kim was my father. He found redemption in Jessica's compassion.

Kim's journey, guided by that compassion, stands as a powerful testament to the transformative impact of second chances. Reflecting on Jessica's life and my father's transformation, we understand more deeply the profound effect of empathy, belief, and opportunity. Jessica's work at the Brotherhood of St. Laurence wasn't just about charity; it was a demonstration of her unwavering belief in the inherent potential within each individual, regardless of their past.

Today, in a society in which a significant portion of the population has experienced incarceration, our attitude toward second-chance hiring is more critical than ever. It transcends the realm of compassionate action, becoming a vital strategy for fostering diverse, resilient communities. Success stories like my father's are proof of the remarkable achievements possible when individuals are given the opportunity to redefine their lives.

By embracing second-chance hiring, we do more than just fill job vacancies; we honor the legacies of visionaries like Jessica. We acknowledge the untapped potential that lies within every person and recognize that behind every statistic is a human story waiting to unfold. Fostering inclusive environments and providing mentorship doesn't just transform individual lives; it enriches our entire community.

The reality is stark: nearly one in three American adults has a criminal record, a statistic that speaks volumes about the employment and social challenges faced by a vast segment of our population. These individuals, often marginalized because of hiring stigmas, represent a reservoir of potential that remains largely untapped. It's imperative to break down these barriers and to view every individual as capable of success and worthy of opportunity.

Jeffery Korzenik's book *Untapped Talent: How Second Chance Hiring Works for Your Business and the Community* offers countless success stories of formerly incarcerated individuals who have excelled in their careers with appropriate support and an enabling environment. Beyond the realm of employment, these narratives showcase what can be achieved on a broader scale.

By providing second-chance opportunities, employers can address their labor shortages while creating more diverse and inclusive workplaces. Tapping into reentry services for qualified employment candidates, creating job skills training initiatives, and establishing mentorships are practical steps businesses can take.

Tapping the pool of veteran talent

Another wellspring of potential talent to tap into is the pool of veterans. Each year, more than 200,000 men and women are discharged from the US armed forces. Consider that each of these individuals brings a unique set of skills and experiences that are ripe for civilian application. Their unique experiences equip them for strategic thinking and dynamic problem-solving, which are both invaluable in any business setting. Veterans represent a vast yet underleveraged asset for the civilian workforce, capable of bringing diverse perspectives and robust problem-solving skills to any organization. Although some may choose to use their GI Bill benefits to continue their education or retire, most are seeking employment in the civilian economy.

Unfortunately, despite their qualifications, veterans are significantly underemployed compared with nonveteran job seekers. This can be attributed to the challenges that many veterans face in transitioning from military to civilian employment. Although some veterans, such as aircraft mechanics, IT specialists, military police, nurses, and hospital lab technicians, can find closely related functions in the civilian world, many others have trouble matching their unique competencies and experience with the needs of civilian employers. If companies were to focus on targeted corporate strategies to harness veterans' discipline and leadership, all parties would benefit.

One of the key challenges facing transitioning military personnel is determining which industries are growing and identifying the companies that are leaders in hiring veterans. In addition to offering job search resources and programs to veterans, employers can also explore apprenticeships for transitioning service members. Doing so is easier than ever thanks to the congressional support now available. Apprenticeships present a practical pathway for veterans to transition into civilian roles, particularly in sectors like transportation, which is facing worker shortages. The magnitude of the diesel technician shortage in the United States is creating significant challenges for the transportation industry. With an estimated 80,000 job vacancies and an additional 28,000 expected openings each year until 2030, the gap between supply and demand is widening at an alarming rate. With these options available, veterans can develop their skills and build careers in civilian industries.

Fortunately, there are many programs and online tools available to help veterans with this process already. The government and the business community recognize the value of the veteran workforce and have made significant efforts to help veterans make the transition to civilian employment. Companies like Boeing, Lockheed Martin, and General Motors are known for actively recruiting veterans. However, despite these efforts, the employment rates for veterans in their first year after leaving the armed forces are less than stellar. While some find immediate employment, others face challenges due to the gap between military and civilian workplace cultures, struggle to get recognition of their skills, and/or find they need additional training or certification.

Furthermore, many veterans face underemployment, meaning they are employed in positions that do not fully utilize their skills or provide adequate compensation. This issue is more prevalent in the veteran community than for their nonveteran counterparts. Underemployment represents not just a loss for veterans but a missed opportunity for industries in dire need of the unparalleled skills that veterans offer.

Incorporating veterans into the workforce is not just a hiring decision but a strategic investment. They bring to the table a set of unique experiences, and their military training makes them adaptable problem-solvers who work well under pressure. They have often developed strong leadership skills through their military service and are effective team managers in civilian workplaces. If that's not enough, veterans also generally possess a strong work ethic, personal responsibility, and maturity, making them reliable in roles that require critical thinking, attention to detail, and decision-making skills. It's these core attributes that make veterans not just employees but invaluable assets for fostering a culture of resilience and excellence within any organization.

Hiring a veteran not only benefits the individual employer; it also contributes to the greater good of society by providing meaningful employment opportunities to those who have served their country. I've witnessed firsthand the unparalleled skills, dedication, and value they bring to our workforce. I'm proud to employ veterans in my company.

Lifelong learning and skill verification in the digital age

In today's marketplace, lifelong learning has become essential for both leaders and their teams to stay ahead of the curve. Skills—both digital and nondigital—aren't just driving the economy; they're reshaping it. As a leader, you need to ensure that your team's skills are not just current but also verifiable. Digital passports are a game-changer here. In essence, a digital skills passport is an online document or profile that showcases a candidate's skills and qualifications. It serves as a continuous record of each employee's skill development and is helpful for connecting skilled talent to potential employers. Everywhere you look, from manufacturing to marketing, the demand for digital savvy is sky-rocketing. Reflecting this growing trend, an Ipsos survey found that roughly 91 percent of employees value personalized training, and 93 percent prefer training that's easy to understand and complete.[1] These numbers not only underscore the value of employee training but also emphasize the pressing need for organizations to invest in effective, accessible, and continuous learning solutions.

The bigger picture reveals a compelling narrative: companies invest-ing in comprehensive training programs see marked benefits—not just in employee morale or satisfaction but in tangible business out-comes like higher income per employee and improved profit margins. Investing in your people has gone from being a nice extra to an absolute must in your business strategy.

Digital passports are particularly beneficial for smaller and mid-sized companies, empowering them to track and showcase their team's growing competencies. This capability is crucial as these companies increasingly turn to online courses, partnerships with educational insti-tutions, and targeted in-house training to boost their workforce's skills. (Refer to the Appendix for a comprehensive list of platforms.) These offerings are essential to cultivating a culture of continuous growth and adaptability and for developing skilled workers to fill the global talent shortage.

Additionally, when smaller companies in sectors like solar energy partner with organizations like the Solar Energy Industries Association (SEIA), the use of digital skills passports becomes invaluable. For example, a young professional enhancing their skills through SEIA's resources can have each new competency authenticated in their digital passport, showcasing their value to current and potential employers.

Through partnerships and training, they gain specialized skills, each of which is authenticated and added to their digital passport. It's a win-win: individuals showcase their ever-growing capabilities while companies align talents with evolving industry needs.

Digital passports are more than just skill trackers; they're empowerment tools. They bridge the gap between skill acquisition and industry recognition, turning every learning opportunity into a potential career milestone. In the digital age, these passports encourage proactive learning, validate achievements, and open doors to new opportunities, ensuring that our workforce isn't just prepared for the future but is actively shaping it.

Utilizing toolkits from organizations like the Interstate Renewable Energy Council (IREC) can also be transformative. IREC's Registered Apprenticeships Toolkit for Clean Energy Employers provides comprehensive guidance for companies to develop skilled workforces. This is all part of "new energy," a term that describes innovations in technology and emerging energy sources that are redefining the industry. By leveraging these external resources, companies don't just invest in individual growth but also contribute to shaping the industry's future.

The pursuit of growth

Before one can pursue growth, it important to define what growth means for employees. Growth is no longer just about climbing the proverbial ladder; it's about expanding horizons and taking on new challenges. I saw this in action with a team leader who stepped out of her comfort zone to lead a project she never thought she could. Her success story and her willingness to take on the challenge inspired the whole team.

Professional development is the cornerstone of career success. Even if you are happy in your current job situation, there's always room for personal improvement. Engaging in activities outside of your comfort zone can be the key to unlocking a new level of success in life and at work. Professional development can open up new opportunities, expand your knowledge of industry trends, build confidence, and increase your perceived value within the workforce. It also helps you feel good—even great—about yourself.

Reaching new heights

Setting goals can be a powerful tool. Goals provide structure and direction, helping to focus energy on what is important to achieve success. People feel rewarded by the process of breaking larger goals into smaller steps and seeing those steps through to completion. This momentum can bring motivation and encouragement during difficult times, when it may seem like a goal is too far out of reach. It's also important to personalize your goals—make them realistic, achievable, and, most of all, meaningful! It will bolster your efforts to act and make positive strides towards achieving your dreams.

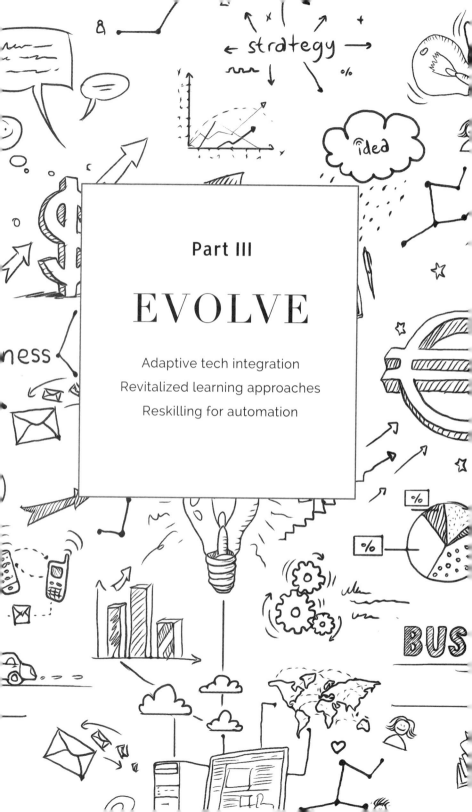

Part III

EVOLVE

Adaptive tech integration
Revitalized learning approaches
Reskilling for automation

CHAPTER 10

Reskill, Reboot, and Refresh

———

THINK OF DIVING INTO THE FUTURE OF WORK AS YOU would think about baking bread from scratch. It only takes a few basics—flour, water, yeast, and salt—but the quality of the loaf depends on how you mix these ingredients, the environment you bake it in, and how you adapt the process to the conditions. Similarly, the future job market requires a mix of skills, learning environments, and adaptability to rise to the occasion—no pun intended!

Embracing the future of work requires a shift in thinking; it's about intentional, strategic upskilling and reskilling. Technology is reshaping the job market, unveiling new job opportunities in its wake. At the start of the twenty-first century, who could have envisioned that new jobs such as podcaster, gamification marketing analyst, digital reputation defender, cloud architect, or mobile app developer would exist? The world is changing, and jobs are changing with it.

I am now actively working on new and emerging jobs with organizations in the clean energy sector, for example. The solar energy industry has now created more than two hundred sixty thousand new jobs across the United States, and there is no sign of that slowing down.

Embracing AI

Despite the often-discussed cost-cutting benefits of AI, companies are slowly embracing AI and leveraging it to not only streamline operations but to innovate and generate new revenue streams. These organizations, diverging from traditional applications, are embedding AI in product development and risk management. Take TiVo's AI initiatives, for example, which have dramatically reduced IT incidents, thus enhancing operational efficiency. Or consider the Einstein Voice Assistant from Salesforce, which is revolutionizing sales processes by automating routine tasks, allowing employees to concentrate on higher-value interactions. These examples illustrate AI's potential not just to improve efficiency but to assist in business growth and innovation.

But should we be worried about AI and how far this may go? The next insight might just do the trick. What if there were a world where, uninterrupted, AI's prowess could eclipse human capability across the board—we're talking about AI outperforming humans in every task imaginable. Although such futuristic predictions make for first-rate sci-fi movies, sources agree that by 2027, AI will gain just 10 percent more capabilities. However, and here's the kicker, these number are expected to balloon to 50 percent by 2047. No, this isn't a speculative sci-fi plot; it's the collective prediction of 2,778 researchers at the forefront of AI, mulling over scenarios from folding laundry to wiring homes.[1]

It comes as no surprise that employers are eager to hire individuals with AI expertise, and they are willing to offer higher salaries to attract such talent. A recent survey conducted by Amazon Web

Services (AWS), in collaboration with Access Partnership, gathered insights from 3,297 employees and 1,340 organizations in the United States and found that IT workers with AI skills could see a salary increase of 47 percent.[2] This trend isn't limited to the tech industry. Salary increases are expected in various departments for those with AI skills, including a 43 percent rise in sales and marketing; 42 percent in finance; 37 percent in legal, regulatory, and compliance; and 35 percent in human resources. These numbers highlight how AI is currently integrating into many aspects of industry and how AI will impact business going forward.

Back to baking that bread. I know artisan bakeries who charge $15 for a loaf of bread, and people happily pay that price. Why? High-quality ingredients, well-trained bakers, and technology that lets buyers know exactly (to the minute) when the bread was made all factor into the higher cost of an "upmarket" loaf of bread.

Rebooting and refreshing

The influx of AI into the business world demonstrates the need to reboot and refresh the training of existing employees. When we talk about workforce development, terms like "reskilling," "upskilling," "continuous learning," and "training" are often used interchangeably, yet they have distinct nuances.

Of those terms, "reskilling" and "upskilling" are most precise, yet each refers to something different. Reskilling is about learning entirely new skills for different roles, especially when one's current job faces obsolescence due to tech advancements. Upskilling, in contrast, is about deepening existing skills to boost proficiency and adaptability in one's current role, often in the wake of new technologies or methodologies. It's essentially bringing people up to speed with the new ways of work and the latest tools of technology.

Consider AT&T and the company's comprehensive $1 billion initiative, known as Future Ready, to educate its workforce. This program is designed to reskill and prepare employees for the evolving digital economy, covering areas such as cybersecurity, data science, and more.

Microsoft provides another example and has committed to providing AI skilling opportunities to 2 million people in India by 2025, focusing on smaller cities and rural areas.

Opportunity is knocking. It's also possible that upskilling and reskilling initiatives will set you up to tap into new markets. The more versatile your workers, the more areas of business you can explore.

Unlocking AI: transforming workforce potential

AI has clearly made its way into the working world with a splash, and its emergence may cause a tidal wave for some industries. Let's delve into the key ingredients of AI and explore its impact on you and the world of work.

The demand for AI skills is now significantly reshaping hiring practices and salary structures across diverse industries. That AWS survey I mentioned earlier notes that 73 percent of employers are actively seeking individuals with AI skills, signaling a significant change in what is considered essential expertise in today's workforce. However, finding these skilled individuals presents a challenge for about three-quarters of these employers. This highlights a need to address the current shortage of available AI professionals, which is not surprising considering how quickly AI moved from sci-fi to reality.

Ten years ago, my company hired an in-house graphic designer skilled in using Adobe InDesign, considered the ultimate design tool at the time. However, it proved to be complex and intimidating software for individuals like me who lacked an understanding of graphic design. Nowadays, we no longer solely rely on this designer for our design needs. Instead, we leverage AI and other technologies to assist us in creating visually appealing professional designs.

Unbeknownst to me, around the same time, a small startup called Canva emerged as a disruptive force within the traditional design realm by making graphic design accessible to everyone, regardless of their level of experience. Canva simplifies the design process with a drag-and-drop interface and an extensive collection of templates and design elements. It is one of those great success stories of startups in which a small, innovative company enters an industry dominated by more advanced professional tools, such as Adobe Photoshop and Illustrator, and offers a more user-friendly and cost-effective alternative. This approach has opened up the design world to a broader audience, including small business owners, educators, students, and professionals from nondesign backgrounds. The rise and integration of AI have greatly enhanced Canva's capabilities.

Canva changed the game for my designer. At first, he didn't want anyone to know he was using it. One day, I mentioned it to him, and he said, "Shhhh, don't tell anyone—or I'll be laughed out of my job." The once indispensable expertise of the designer could now be replicated with just a few clicks. No longer was he the sole creator and gatekeeper of all our designs. However, this microcosm of change reflected a more significant trend. Our graphic designer remained in his role and used AI tools to produce high-quality, professional designs more efficiently. Like so many people, he was now collaborating closely with technology.

Today, he finds himself at the control panel of technology on which he can make incredible graphics that were not possible even a few years ago. It's important to remember that creative minds keep on thinking up great ideas, and the technology simply makes them easier to accomplish.

Ethical AI in the workplace: no pie in the sky

Let's face it—the shift towards integrating AI into our workplaces isn't without significant challenges. It's not just about unlocking efficiency or sparking innovation; it's also a tightrope walk over an ethical chasm. While we are now deep into the digital age, company managers and leaders find themselves carefully steering this precarious journey. Here are some of the dangers to watch for:

Bias in AI: AI algorithms are only as worldly as the data they are trained on. For that reason, we need a rich tapestry of diverse data to avoid AI biases that can skew decision-making. Biases don't just make you look bad; they're bad business and can be bad for your bottom line. Diversifying data, sources of data, and those choosing data to input into AI systems isn't just ethical; it's smart. It ensures that your AI tools are sharp and reliable. Remember: technology is based on who is programming it—AI included. Therefore, if someone is programming AI based on biases or unsubstantiated information, AI will not provide the quality level of insight you need.

Clear as glass: Transparency about AI's role and impact in your organization builds trust. It's like being clear about the ingredients in a dish: people want to know what they're consuming. Similarly, employees deserve to understand how AI might affect their roles and the way they do their job. The assumption that AI has all the right answers is very common but may be very wrong. In other words, people need to know how AI is being originated and used, especially in decisions that effect them and/or their livelihood.

Use AI to elevate: Use AI to upskill, reskill, and save valuable time for your workforce. Think of AI as a chef's knife: in the right hands, it enhances creativity and efficiency; unused, it's just another tool in the drawer.

A dash of Davos: The buzz around AI at Davos, where the World Economic Forum is held, highlights its global impact. But let's not get lost in the hype. The real takeaway? Thoughtful AI integration is not about keeping up with the Joneses (i.e., your competitors) but about growing your business in an efficient but ethical and sustainable way.

AI Takeaways

- **Audit your ai:** Conduct regular checks to ensure that your AI systems work as intended without infringing on privacy or exhibiting bias.

- **Educate your team:** Knowledge is power. Ensure your employees understand AI's role in your business and their careers.

- **Foster innovation with integrity:** Encourage that your team to explore AI's potential responsibly. Let them be the architects of your AI journey, grounded in ethical practices.

- **Stay informed:** The AI landscape is constantly evolving. Keep abreast of the latest developments, regulatory guidelines, and ethical standards to ensure that your business remains within the bounds of responsible AI use.

- Always remember, and remind others, that AI does NOT have all the answers; it is rooted in human programming.

In navigating the ethical integration of AI in the workplace, some might say we're reaching for a "pie in the sky"—a term that implies lofty ambitions that are hard to achieve. It is also the name of a popular British TV series in which Detective Inspector Henry Crabbe not only cracks cases but also pours his heart into running a restaurant called Pie in the Sky, known for its gastronomy. Although it was certainly not akin to AI, it was full of ethical dilemmas (not to mention witty British dialogue and plenty of fresh, locally grown produce).

A few words about security in the twenty-first century

If you're going to have a successful business, you must protect it like it's your job (because it is). Employee data protection isn't just a box to check. Everyone needs to be well aware of the fragility of your business when it comes to breaches of personal records, be it employees, vendors, customers, or anyone else with data stored somewhere in your company's technology or in the cloud.

There are courses, seminars, consultants, experts, websites, and books that provide a wealth of knowledge about cybersecurity. Make security part of your employee training. It is essential for any twenty-first-century workforce to learn and utilize the latest tools for data security management.

The need to create and enact security policies and include firewalls, encryption, antivirus software, and various other technical tools to help keep your business safe has become common practice in business today. You may find yourself hiring a chief information security officer (CISO). Bottom line: if you're going to be in business, protect your business and your workforce.

Prescription for a strong economy

This skills shortage will only continue to get worse in the years ahead as the baby boomer generation (people born between 1946 and 1964) move into retirement, taking their experience and technical know-how with them. Couple this with many companies still engaging in ageism, pushing people out the door in their fifties, and you find too few skilled workers able to integrate the tried-and-true knowledge culled from experience with the new technology of today. As a result, too many promising new projects are left on the shelf.

In manufacturing, it is now estimated that by 2030, there will be 2.1 million unfulfilled jobs due to a lack of skilled labor. Another industry that has been experiencing a critical workforce shortage is construction. In 2024, the industry needed an estimated 501,000 additional workers beyond the normal hiring rate to meet labor demands. This shortage was compounded by the high level of job openings in the industry, averaging more than 390,000 per month in 2022, the highest on record.

No question, there is also a shortage of workers in industries like healthcare, in which an inadequate supply of college-trained people—particularly scientists, doctors, and engineers—account for part of the skills gap.

However, most of the positions that need to be filled today and in the future do not require a college degree. They can be handled successfully by "middle-skilled" individuals, those with a high school diploma plus an associate degree or an apprenticeship.

Yet given the number of young people in the labor pipeline who are achieving those levels, many positions will still not be filled. Governments are aware of the issue, but, with all due respect, if companies wait for governments to fix this problem, they may be waiting a long time. A thriving economy needs a robust workforce of people with all sorts of skills and training: electricians, chefs, trained mechanics, machinists, welders, plumbers, horticulturalists, carpenters, customer service personnel, caterers, lab and healthcare workers, solar energy installers, and literally thousands of other occupations.

That said, governments do have a role to play. They need to create an environment in which employers are motivated to jump-start some of these human capital programs. Such programs forge an important link between school and the world of work. It's simply good policy. I mean, what government wants people leaving school and sitting idle on the sidelines, unemployed and disengaged? Wouldn't they much rather invest a little to help people transition smoothly from school to respectable employment? (Not to mention, doing so creates more taxpayers!)

CHAPTER 11

Revolutionizing Workforce Education

———

WE'VE BEEN COLLECTIVELY ENTRANCED BY THE MANTRA "college for all," convinced that a traditional four-year college degree is the starting point for achieving a prosperous, secure professional future. And let's not even get into the push for grad school. Yet reality paints a more complex, often less rosy picture.

Over the last decade, American faith in higher education has plummeted, marking a growing skepticism towards these once-esteemed academic institutions. Data from a Gallup poll reveal that the proportion of individuals harboring considerable confidence in higher education institutions has dipped from 57 percent in 2015 to a mere 36 percent in more recent years.[1]

And let's not overlook the substantial price of obtaining a four-year diploma. As of 2024, the burden of student debt in the United States has swollen to an astronomical $1.74 trillion. This staggering statistic is a testament to the crushing weight of dreams deferred, if not defeated, under financial strain. To truly grasp this amount, consider that a trillion dollars is a thousand billion, or a million million.

The number of digits on student debt doesn't even fit on a calculator: $1,740,000,000,000. It's a figure so high that its sheer magnitude is challenging to fully comprehend, reflecting the profound and pervasive financial burden of higher education on countless individuals.

The notion of a one-size-fits-all college education seems increasingly out of touch when you consider the fact that people possess a huge range of different knowledge, skill sets, and interests. In addition, people learn in many ways. Some people simply do not thrive in a traditional classroom environment, focused on highly academic pursuits that require lots of study over lots of years. Some are skilled with their hands. And many equally intelligent individuals are just as passionate about building airplanes, or a career in robotics, as someone chasing down a law degree. While some people have lofty ambitions to become doctors, even surgeons, is it any less noble to dream of making a difference in the world as an emergency medical technician, a home healthcare worker, or a social entrepreneur? We all have different passions, talents, and ambitions. So why are we expected to follow the same educational path? The old way of thinking suggests that college is the answer for everyone; clearly, that's no longer true when you consider how many success stories come from people who did not graduate college. Just look at Bill Gates, Steve Jobs, Larry Ellison, Rachael Ray, and Walt Disney. You may have heard of them.

Recent controversies have also significantly challenged higher education. Issues ranging from unfair college admissions practices to allegations of prejudice within academic leadership have not only caused ripples across college campuses but have fundamentally altered the academic landscape. These challenges signal a need for a deep reassessment of the principles, transparency, and inclusivity of our educational institutions.

The entrenched "college for all" belief is once again under scrutiny. A 2023 study by the University of Chicago and the *Wall Street Journal* found that 56 percent of Americans feel that a four-year college degree isn't worth it.[2] The sentiments expressed by readers echo my belief that although college can be an invaluable experience for some, it is not the universal destination it was once heralded to be.

In 2024, two research companies looked at a dataset of 60 million Americans in the US job market to see how recent college graduates fared. The results, from the Burning Glass Institute and the Strada Institute for Future Work, showed that most graduates between 2012 and 2021 were working in fields that did not require a college degree. In fact, 53 percent of recent four-year college graduates were found to be underemployed.[3]

The dilemma extends beyond the financial strain of four-year schools; it raises questions about the relevance, practicality, and true value of these degrees in today's rapidly evolving world. Matt Sigelman, president of the Burning Glass Institute, writes about a groundswell of "voices seeking to demand that higher education justify its value."[4] Meanwhile, Jon Marcus writes in the nonprofit The Hechinger Report about how "higher education has lost its shine" with the perception that costs have become uncontrollable. He says colleges don't show clear links "between academic disciplines and careers or keep up with the demands of the fast-moving labor market."[5] "The traditional four-year degree is losing its shine," writes another observer.

For those certain about a career path that requires a graduate or professional degree, college is the route to take. For these students, whose vision is crystal clear and whose aspirations align precisely with their chosen field, college isn't just a step; it's a monumental leap towards realizing their dreams.

However, for many people, alternate routes like apprenticeships or vocational training provide a more direct and fulfilling journey to career success. In the computer and tech sector, many self-taught programmers have also used coding boot camps, software engineering courses, and free online resources to learn programming.

Personally, I've navigated this discussion with my daughter, Alexandra (Alex), who walks the campus of a traditional college, a fact that might raise eyebrows considering my advocacy for career technical education (CTE) paths. But here's where the narrative becomes more nuanced. These decisions are a reflection not just of personal choices but of the broader discussion of educational pathways.

To set the record straight, I'm not advocating college for no one. It's quite the opposite. I'm advocating for the right education at the right time for the right person. Far from universally dismissing colleges, I assert that the decision to embark on the journey of higher education must be intimately driven by the student's genuine passion and intention.

Alex was captivated by some of her college's unconventional offerings and drawn to the innovative spirit that characterizes the campus. Her choice, though different from mine, illustrates the diversity of educational paths, each valuable in its own right.

It's time to embrace a broader view of education, one that values diverse paths and prepares individuals for the multifaceted challenges of the future.

To attract greater enrollment and a more diverse group of learners, some colleges are engaging in new ideas for classes and areas of study. For example, at the University of California, Davis, education goes beyond traditional modes. Students engage in hands-on learning, from cultivating edible mushrooms to exploring the science of coffee brewing. Courses also delve into the relationship between humans and animals, highlighting the university's innovative approach to blending academic study with practical experience.

Institutions like UC Davis are not just adapting; they're leading an educational renaissance. Drawing from my own unconventional educational journey, I firmly believe it's time for us to broaden our perspectives and wholeheartedly embrace the diverse educational paths that will equip our modern workforce for the future's demands.

Educational stigmas

Why do we mythologize American entrepreneurship and laud American advances in technological innovation, yet our secondary educational system lags behind that of virtually all other developed nations in terms of integrating computer science, engineering, and other technical competencies into their core curricula?

Why does this old-school stigma against vocational and technical learning stubbornly hang on? Why do parents announce their child's plans to attend a polytechnic institute or community college less loudly and proudly than they would their child's acceptance to a third- or fourth-tier college, let alone an elite one?

My own career offers an example of how developing a marketable skill through nontraditional education can set a young person on a rewarding and successful pathway through life. When I left high school, much to the chagrin of my family and guidance counselor, I had just begun a culinary apprenticeship in the kitchen of a popular five-star hotel. I knew in my heart that college was not where I belonged at that point in my life. And yet my parents were both well-meaning and flexible. They soon envisioned a different path for their son. It was, however, not an easy path. In fact, I had almost given up on my dream to become a chef, until Sandro Brunelli came into the picture. He was an Italian restaurateur from my old neighborhood who gave me some much-needed advice and arranged work experience at his world-renowned Campari Bistro. After proving myself in the kitchens of an international hotel, I secured a job as a fish chef at a London restaurant that would go on to earn a coveted Michelin star. This is my mantra: never give up. Sometimes, life's script has a twist waiting just around the corner, and all it takes is that one person, one opportunity, to turn the whole story around. Isn't that just the spice of life?

This experience taught me the invaluable lesson that success isn't always found in traditional classrooms. Sometimes, it's down the path laid out by mentors and real-world experiences. And never underestimate the power of pursuing your passion.

Why hands-on learning is essential for success

A *Forbes* magazine article I wrote entitled "'Why We Desperately Need to Bring Back Vocational Training in Schools" not only sparked debate but also went viral (well, viral for a workforce article, in any case), attracting more than 2 million views and countless comments. This piece didn't just strike a chord; it hit a nerve, sparking a widespread and lasting conversation. But what exactly about this article made it such a viral sensation?

Let's start with my use of the word "vocational" in the headline. I was walking down Third Avenue in Manhattan when I got a call on my cell phone from an unknown number; I answered, and on the other end was a spirited caller strongly advising me to steer clear of using the word "vocational" again because of its negative connotations. Honestly, at first, I thought it was a recording, but then I wondered how an automated system would know I had used that word in an article. It turned out that it was the White House chair of the Committee on Education and the Workforce. I'm glad she called me out on using "the V word" (vocational), and I proceeded to visit D.C. several times to discuss workforce policy.

Why is the V word off limits? It's a term that has mistakenly been equated with low-skilled labor by some—I get it. To set the record straight, a friend in Germany described it like this: leave off the last two letters—"vocation(al)"—and you get "vocation," a term that should be celebrated for its focus on skilled, purposeful work.

So what (apart from my use of "vocational") sparked nearly 2 million people to read the article and caused many to get so worked up?

The piece opened a dialogue about the importance of hands-on learning. People want to do things with both their heads and their hands. For decades, high school students in the United States were taught academic subjects (e.g., reading, writing, and arithmetic) along with vocational skills (e.g., woodwork or metalwork) in shop class. However, in the 1950s, a new philosophy emerged, separating students into different educational tracks based on their abilities. This led to vocational education being perceived as a lower track for minority and working-class students and consequently being removed from the academic core. The focus shifted to preparing all students for college regardless of their passions or goals.

Consider that 68 percent of high school students attend college, but 40 percent don't complete their four-year degree programs, wasting time and money while accumulating student loan debt. Despite college programs not suiting many students, states still continue cutting vocational/CTE programs, limiting educational options.

We should be recognizing and celebrating the incredible educators that continue to shape our world by investing in public education. Unfortunately, too many teachers are being hindered from reaching their full potential because of cumbersome bureaucracy. It's crucial to cut bureaucratic red tape and empower educators to fully unlock the potential in each student.

How can you bring the entrepreneurial spirit to your workplace? Discover the secrets to unlocking your employees' drive through dynamic and unique learning methods tailored to individual learning styles. Embrace innovative learning and entrepreneurial thinking in your workplace. This approach goes beyond skill building; it's about sparking a lifelong passion for learning and discovery.

CHAPTER 12

Unlocking Excellence

———

DESPITE THE PRESSURE OFTEN PLACED ON CEOS TO DELIVER short-term gains, the real key to a company's long-term success is investing in employee skills and retention. It's become evident that firms prioritizing skills development and nurturing their talent are the ones scripting their own narratives of long-term triumph. It's high time that pay structures and incentives reflect this broader, more sustainable vision of success.

Consider Cisco and Unilever, both of which, like many large companies, focus on the benefits of prioritizing skills development and employee retention. Cisco's initiative, the Cisco Learning Network, empowers its workforce with cutting-edge technological training, a spectrum of professional development courses, and robust leadership cultivation programs. Similarly, Unilever has implemented the Unilever Future Leaders Program, a two-year graduate program that provides participants with the opportunity to work on real business projects and develop leadership skills. By investing in employee training and development, these companies are creating a culture of innovation and creativity and attracting and retaining top talent.

In this digital age, the proliferation of online training, now a $400 billion industry, showcases our dedication to continuous learning. And these training courses aren't just made up of slide decks and recorded lectures. They make use of innovative technologies like virtual reality (VR), exemplified by Transfr VR, a company I recently discovered at a career expo that helps organizations train students for the workforce using immersive learning experiences that go beyond traditional boundaries.

VR, once just a gaming tool, now enhances education in colleges and industry, at companies like Mazda Toyota Manufacturing for training workers on how to operate the automotive painting robots. It's a safer and more efficient alternative to working on potentially dangerous machinery and can be applied across many fields. Think chemical handling, firefighting, military operations, and electrical work.

But online training and VR aren't just for those handling dangerous tasks. Beyond specialized fields like healthcare or IT, immersive learning is also available for a wide range of subjects, including languages, marketing, leadership, and more. For example, I've also started taking Spanish lessons on Duolingo. The app offers short, daily lessons that are both fun and effective.

As we move into the next era of innovation, watch for the rise of extended reality (XR) as it merges VR and augmented reality to enhance virtual meetings and digital collaboration. XR is narrowing the divide between physical and virtual workspaces, enhancing remote interactions. This isn't just speculation; it could become a tangible part of the work process, reshaping how we connect and work remotely. Imagine being in a virtual meeting that feels as real as being there in person.

While online training equips individuals with cutting-edge skills, it's also instrumental in addressing the broader economic challenges we face today. The rapid shifts in workforce dynamics necessitate a robust approach to cultivating a resilient and adaptable labor force. This is where the significance of middle-skilled labor comes into sharp focus, representing a vital cog in the machinery of our economy.

By ensuring that our workforce is skilled and adaptable, we not only address immediate labor shortages but also lay the groundwork for long-term economic stability. In this context, it's instructive to consider the exemplary practices of companies like Southwest Airlines, which illustrates the profound impact of strategic employee retention and skills development on corporate success.

Prioritizing skills development and employee retention isn't just ethical; it's a smart business strategy for enduring success.

Harnessing the power of mentorship

Oprah Winfrey put it succinctly: "A mentor is someone who allows you to see the hope inside yourself." Indeed, mentors aren't just guides; they're the lighthouses that illuminate our potential, inspiring a surge of newfound confidence and broadening our horizons.

There I was, a young chef in the back hallway of the Regent Hotel, when I saw a bread roll on the floor. For some inexplicable reason, perhaps a brain fart, instead of picking it up, I impulsively kicked it. Little did I know, this lapse in judgment was about to earn me a significant lesson in professionalism and attention to detail, thanks to Mr. Markl, the general manager, who happened to see my attempt to score a soccer goal with a bread roll.

Mr. Markl quickly retrieved the roll before turning around and reading my name badge out loud. "Nicholas Wyman, Apprentice

Chef," he said, followed swiftly by, "Ah, our new apprentice, please join me at 10:00 sharp tomorrow morning in my office." My heart sank as I imagined the worst.

When I stepped into the GM's office the next morning, after a night of little sleep and much worrying, an atmosphere of quiet sophistication greeted me. A fine-dining waiter, impeccably dressed in a crisp black-and-white uniform, was meticulously arranging an elegant morning tea setup in the lounge area of Mr. Markl's expansive office. Behind his desk, Mr. Markl observed the scene with an attentive eye. The spread of aromatic coffee and exquisite French pastries, I assumed, must be for an important meeting to follow.

However, to my surprise, Mr. Markl gestured invitingly towards me. "Mr. Wyman, please, join me," he beckoned, his voice turning my apprehension into a blend of curiosity and unexpected gratitude. As we shared the morning tea, his passion for the hospitality industry was palpable and infectious, igniting a similar fervor within me. His conversation was not just talk; it was an engaging narrative of his own early days in the world of hospitality, filled with insights and lessons.

As I was about to leave, Mr. Markl shared a simple yet profound lesson. With a firm yet gentle tone, he said, "When we see something on the floor, Mr. Wyman, we pick it up—yes?" The simplicity of his words belied their profound impact, encapsulating the essence of attentiveness and responsibility crucial in hospitality. The lesson was clear, and with a respectful nod, I thought, "Got that!" and then thanked him and went back to work.

That morning, within the walls of Mr. Markl's office, the gap between the top and bottom rungs of the hotel's hierarchy seemed to diminish. It was a moment of genuine mentorship, a testament to the power of guidance, inspiration, and the shared pursuit of excellence in the demanding, yet rewarding, world of hospitality.

Skills on display: the culinary Olympics

Win or lose, a little competition can be a marvelous hands-on learning experience and career booster. Pursuing my dreams catapulted me beyond traditional education into a decade filled with rich experiences in hospitality and tourism, a highlight of which was getting to represent Australia at the Culinary Olympics in Frankfurt, Germany. This was no ordinary cooking competition; it was the Olympiade der Köche, where the finest chefs from around the globe gathered every four years to showcase their skills and creativity.

My team's courageous choice of featuring rabbit in our dish was just the beginning of an exciting and challenging adventure at the Culinary Olympics. Our major sponsor, the Australian Dried Fruits Association, insisted we incorporate dried fruits into our dish, forcing us to explore uncharted culinary combinations. We focused on the sweet and tangy apricots for their versatility. This led us to create a dish we called Desert Bloom, with the unusual combination of savory rabbit and the sweetness of dried apricots, evoking the feel of Australia.

Now, fast forward a few decades and enter with me the realm of the visionary chef Heston Blumenthal, a name synonymous with molecular gastronomy (the scientific approach of cuisine from the perspective of chemistry). His renowned restaurant, Dinner by Heston Blumenthal, in London, pays homage to the depths of British gastronomy, breathing new life into ancient recipes with a modern twist.

Speaking of Heston, I had quite the adventure in Provence. Planning to visit Eygalières, where Heston often retreats, I ended up in Eyguières because of my fair but imperfect French. As I parked and wandered around Eyguières, thinking it was the right spot, my daughter, Alexandra, pointed out, "Dad, we've missed the mark by three villages!" Eyguières, while lovely, just didn't have that culinary vibe. Lesson learned: always double-check the spelling, especially in Provence.

Chef Heston Blumenthal is celebrated for his mastery of molecular gastronomy.

I did, however, manage to find my way to his London restaurant, where I sampled one his most iconic dishes, the Meat Fruit. Resembling a small mandarin in appearance, it surprises, as it's actually chicken liver parfait encased in mandarin jelly. The Meat Fruit showcases Heston's knack for blending the past with the present, and a touch of science, while creating amazing dishes that also taste great. The origins of Meat Fruit trace back to medieval times, when food was not just nourishment but also a spectacle and a surprise. These elaborate feasts often featured similar meat fruits as a remarkable example of *entremets*—courses designed to entertain and astonish guests. These dishes were disguised as one thing but revealed a completely different and surprising filling—in this case, a fruit filled with meat.

When creating Desert Bloom, we had no idea about the history of meat and fruit. In any case, it was a winner on the day. We picked up the Luxembourg lion trophy and brought home a gold medal for Australia.

Switzerland

Success at the Culinary Olympics opened doors that led to many amazing opportunities, including an international scholarship to study at Ecole Hôtelière de Lausanne Switzerland, one of the oldest hotel schools in the world. As a student there, I didn't just sit through classroom-style lectures; we had successful entrepreneurs from the industry, like Swiss chef Anton Mosimann teaching us the tricks of the trade. Chef Mosimann is a star in the food scene and former maître chef de cuisines at London's Dorchester Hotel, where he received two Michelin awards. He invented the Cuisine Naturelle style of cooking, which puts prime importance on fresh ingredients and light seasoning. And more recently, he did the catering for a wedding reception for a lovely English couple, Will and Kate—now the Prince and Princess of Wales, future King and Queen of England.

The Ecole Hôtelière classes were full of hotel managers and me—the only chef! It gave me an instant connection with Chef Mosimann, and we became lifelong friends. It was one of those right place, right time things. I do remember some early mentoring he provided me: "Nick, don't wait for your ship to come in; swim out to it."

Successful mentor–mentee relationships

A successful mentoring relationship is fundamentally built on trust and respect between mentor and mentee. Mentors need to be patient and provide feedback while also knowing when to step back and allow mentees to lead projects and tasks.

Open-mindedness is crucial; both mentor and mentee should be ready to listen and learn from each other without judgment. The best scenario comes from establishing an environment open for questions, shared experiences, and constructive criticism that benefits both mentor and mentee.

Success in mentoring also comes from recognizing and valuing each other's unique talents, strengths, and weaknesses. It's also important for both parties to know what they don't know, meaning that they recognize a need to learn in specific areas. Historical pairs like Oprah Winfrey and Maya Angelou, Benjamin Franklin and Thomas Jefferson, and Socrates and Plato exemplify the profound impact of mentor–mentee relationships.

Mentoring can happen one-to-many, too. I was part of a medical technology delegation and found myself at the Johnson & Johnson Innovation – JLABS location in Houston, Texas. JLABS is a global network of open innovation ecosystems, supporting and scaling early-stage companies in the pharmaceutical, medical device, consumer, and health tech sectors.

The JLABS facility I toured provides lab space, specialized equipment, and mentorship to startups working in these areas. The goal is to nurture scientific innovation by providing resources and expertise that help these early-stage companies develop their ideas and bring new solutions to market. This support often includes access to scientific, industry, and capital funding experts, as well as opportunities to collaborate with researchers from Johnson & Johnson and other companies.

Building an impactful mentor program

Start your mentorship program with clear objectives: define the skills, topics, and areas of focus. To begin building your program, you'll want to carefully match employees with one or two mentors according to their specific needs and interests, ensuring accessible and relevant guidance.

Consider Janine's mentorship of Charmaine at Esso, transforming her from a supermarket employee to a high-tech industry star. Janine, who had worked with me for many years, had been part of the WPC Group, an intermediary community partner bridging the gap between employers and apprentices for more than forty years. She embodied the essence of a passionate and dedicated mentor.

Charmaine's journey from supermarket employee to electro-technology expert was accelerated by Janine's focused mentorship. Charmaine learned to navigate the complexities of the industry, understand the intricate details of her trade, and build a network of valuable connections.

The impact of this mentorship was profound. Charmaine's skills and confidence grew exponentially, and that was reflected in her work. She became known for her meticulous attention to detail, innovative problem-solving approach, and ability to work seamlessly with the team. The mentorship journey culminated in a remarkable feat for Charmaine: representing her team at a prestigious industry event, where her skills earned widespread acclaim.

This mentor–mentee relationship didn't just equip Charmaine

with the necessary technical skills. It instilled in her a sense of confidence, a deep understanding of the industry, and, most importantly, the realization that with determination and the right guidance, success is within reach. It was Janine, through her tech knowledge and experience, patience, and guidance, who transformed Charmaine from an apprentice into a rising star in the high-tech industry, underscoring the power of a well-structured mentorship program.

T.R.U.S.T.

Mentorship programs are a great way for employers to motivate people while developing their skill sets at the same time—but only if done right! To establish a successful mentoring program, consider setting clear standards, providing regular feedback, using proven methodologies, fostering strong relationships, developing coaching skills, and monitoring success. Additionally, aim to engage a diverse mentor pool, leading to a more enriching program.

Central to mentoring is T.R.U.S.T.:

- **Transparency:** Foster clear communication and mutual respect.
- **Respect:** Respect each other's experiences and knowledge.
- **Understanding:** Foster open-minded learning and development.
- **Support:** Offer guidance and support throughout the mentee's journey.
- **Time:** Schedule regular check-ins to track progress.

Self-directed learning

Recently, I came across a term you don't hear that often: "heutagogy." It's a fancy way of saying "self-determined learning." The learning style is not sitting back and watching; it's about actively participating. Whilst the term might be new to you, the approach, I'm sure, is not. This method resonates across generations, and maybe it's time to revisit it, take the best parts from your experiences, and include this way of learning in your workplace. Heutagogy 2.0, as it were.

Heutagogy is, of course, just one theory and practice of learning. The evolution of learning tools over centuries has led to diverse learning methods. After all, we learn in different ways and even excel beyond the expectations of society or other people. Consider the story of Helen Keller, the first deaf-blind person to earn a bachelor of arts degree from a major university. Her exceptional story exemplifies how far one can go beyond their perceived boundaries. It's a testament to the multiple avenues of learning available.

Through the teaching of Anne Sullivan, Helen Keller learned to read, write, and speak. In fact, Helen Keller would go on to write books and do speaking engagements, during which she talked about the politics of the era.

When it comes to learning, one size clearly does not fit all. By embracing various learning styles and incorporating different approaches, you can create a learning environment to engage your employees and help them reach their full potential. It's a win-win, for them and the company.

On a recent trip to Palo Alto, California, I went behind the scenes to look at one of the most innovative companies in the fight against cancer, Varian Medical Systems. Walking through Varian's Palo Alto facility, I observed workforce training in a competitive, high-tech environment. Varian, situated in the tech hub of Palo Alto, has to navigate the challenge of attracting and retaining talent in a market dominated by tech giants. At Varian, the emphasis on diverse learning styles was apparent. The facility buzzed with teams engaged in building, servicing, and repairing intricate cancer treatment machinery.

An executive at Varian pointed out, "We look for people with a mix of skills—mechanical experience, electronics background, and even physics knowledge. This blend is crucial for the work we do here, from building to maintaining our complex machines." This outlook aligns with our discussion on the importance of embracing diverse learning styles to drive growth and success.

Commitment to on-the-job training was a key aspect of Varian's strategy. This approach ensured that learning was not just about acquiring skills but adapting them to the unique, ever-changing challenges of people's roles. Varian's dedication to continuous learning mirrored the proactive and engaging styles we advocate for, showing that even in highly technical fields, diverse learning strategies work wonderfully.

Part IV

CONNECT

Strategic talent acquisition
Hybrid workspace innovation
Empowerment through development

CHAPTER 13

Attracting and Hiring Top Talent

———

"YOU NEVER GET A SECOND CHANCE TO MAKE A FIRST impression." In the competitive world of recruitment, this isn't just a catchy phrase; it's reality for employers and candidates alike.

To transcend traditional resume reviews, my team and I utilize "targeted selection" methods, probing candidates to share experiences and stories that illuminate their problem-solving skills and adaptability—key traits that align with our core values and culture.

Let's shift our focus to the how of our hiring process. This chapter is designed to provide actionable insights, real-world applications, and examples of how my company implements the principles of hiring discussed earlier. It's about turning theory into practice and ensuring that our hiring strategies are as effective and impactful as possible.

Gone are the days of tedious resume reviews and grueling interviews. In hiring, it's not just about the skills on paper; it's about the person behind the resume. And on the employer side, I focus on crafting a company brand that resonates with the type of people I want to attract. Like a magnet, it draws in talent that aligns perfectly with our culture and values.

Part of this branding involves shifting interview settings to places like coffee shops, creating a relaxed atmosphere that encourages authenticity and a genuine exchange, allowing us to see beyond the resume and get a feel for the individual's true potential for integration into our team.

Smart employers today prioritize aligning company goals with employee needs. It's about more than just filling positions; it's about creating roles that resonate, encouraging a longer, more fruitful tenure with the company. Remember that most people today work for more than just a paycheck. For employees, it's about finding purpose and meaning and being part of a culture that motivates and encourages them to strive to meet their goals and those of the company.

In our hiring process, we actively seek candidates who not only have the technical skills necessary for the role but also possess the people skills and personal attributes that we discussed in Chapter 3.

To effectively gauge these qualities, we introduce workplace tours and impromptu interactions with team members as part of the interview process. This strategy lets us observe candidates in more natural, unscripted scenarios, providing insights into their interpersonal skills and how they might adapt to our company's environment.

The company with the best talent wins

Making a strong first impression is not only critical for candidates, it is equally important for employers. Additionally, creative hiring outreach techniques can be very helpful for both job seekers and employers to find that perfect match.

I tell my recruitment team that the company with the best talent wins, but talent means more than just technical talent. Alongside technical skills, we look for people skills and certain personal attributes, which can be hard to uncover through a regular interview process. With a team of six professional recruiters, our focus is on practical, standout strategies to attract exceptional talent.

Here are some ways we assess a candidate's talents:

- **Technical skills:** When it comes to checking technical skills for a qualified person, we often need to be creative. For example, when hiring an electrician, it's not like we can bring in a circuit board and watch them work during an interview. Instead, we take a close look at their certifications, qualifications, and past work experience. But we don't just take their word for it. We take a deep dive into references and verify critical qualifications. We are looking for a solid background and proven skills for the job. Now, of course, when hiring an apprentice or entry-level worker whom we will be training on and off the job, we are relying less on technical skills (as they generally have none). Instead, we focus on people skills and attributes. We want to know if whether someone is poised and ready to learn what we have to offer.

- **People skills:** In assessing people skills during interviews, we take a practical approach. We get candidates to paint us a picture. Describe a situation in which you had to deal with a challenging team member who was not meeting their deadlines. How did you address the issue, and what was the outcome? If we are hiring several people in similar roles, we might run group interviews or have an open house. We encourage candidates to introduce themselves to other candidates, making it clear there are multiple jobs and these people may be their future workmates. If a person struggles with this interaction, it suggests they might need more development in people skills. For young people or first-time job seekers with a positive attitude but lacking in experience, we consider offering access to free pre-employment training. This training involves hands-on learning. We have candidates practice walking into a room, introducing themselves to other participants, and engaging in mock interviews with members of our employer network. Even if we don't end up hiring them after the training, we see it as a win to help them develop these skills for their future interviews.

- **Attributes:** In partnership with Patti Dirham, I've developed a simple method to discover a candidate's attributes. In the interview, we show candidates a list of attributes (see my list in Appendix 2) and ask them to pick one or two that they feel best describe them. There's no catch here; there's no wrong answer. Their choices are often enlightening, offering a peek into how they might fit with our team and culture. This approach uncovers their potential strengths and development areas—things you can't always glean from a resume or typical interview questions. It's about understanding the whole person, not just the professional façade.

When evaluating candidates, we focus on their adaptability, resilience, and eagerness for continuous learning, as these traits reflect their potential to adapt and grow within our organization. We look for signs of these personal attributes during interviews. How candidates describe overcoming past challenges or their approach to continuous learning can be very revealing about their potential to thrive and grow with us.

In addition to evaluating technical prowess and interpersonal dynamics, we also address instances of candidate uncertainty by asking them to take a moment to reflect on their fit with the role and our culture. Their initiative regarding their follow-up behavior also acts as a strong indicator of their true interest and compatibility with our values, guiding us towards making informed hiring decisions. Candidates who follow up an interview with a thank-you message and even a question are clearly thinking about the position, whereas candidates whom we never hear from again or do not show such indications are most likely not interested. Remember that if you want something you have to go after it, not wait until it comes to you.

The recruitment team is always trying to move outside the box, so to speak. Jobs boards are a tool but not the main way we connect with potential candidates. For example, we host an industry event, which is a great way to engage with potential employees while they gain valuable insight into what it's like to work in a specific field. Connecting with educational programs, clubs, or associations will also help get the word out about open positions. Above all, prioritize the human element in recruitment. Investing in meaningful, genuine conversations can forge connections that transcend the typical transactional nature of hiring. It puts candidates at ease and allows you to find untapped potential and build lasting relationships.

Traditional hiring messages still work

To attract top talent in today's dynamic workplace, we blend modern methods with time-tested traditional approaches.

Although technology and social media have revolutionized recruitment (to a degree), it is important to recognize that traditional methods, proven over many years, remain indispensable. They provide a foundational touchstone that complements the modern recruitment landscape. So let's travel back to the late 1980s, before the internet played a role in recruitment. Back then, companies relied on newspaper ads, direct mail, and local job fairs to find top talent. And you know what? These methods still work today, with a touch of modern flair. This isn't to say emails and online outreach won't be beneficial, but it all depends on what type of people you are looking for and what kind of job you are offering. For example, corporations may field inquiries from various parts of a country or internationally for remote work or positions at offices around the world. However, if you are looking for a chef for your restaurant in a small town or even a city, why not place some ads in local publications or post a note at the nearest culinary institute?

In our approach to hiring, we believe the involvement of family can also be a great tool. Inviting family into the hiring process during an open house enriches the candidate's experience and aligns them with our company's culture. This inclusion provides a deeper insight into our values and vision, and it's especially meaningful for younger adults. That was exactly the case for me in my younger years.

I was a seventeen-year-old looking to leave high school and secure an apprenticeship. After several setbacks, I was excited to receive an invitation to attend a open house hiring event at the prestigious Regent Hotel. The purpose of this event was to give me (and my parents) an opportunity to learn more about the hotel, the brand, and the vision, as well as to meet people working in the hotel. On arrival, we were warmly greeted and given name badges by HR Director

Graham Burleigh, who welcomed us to join the other prospective apprentices and their families whilst enjoying afternoon tea. He talked about the vision of American hotel tycoon Robert H. Burns, who founded the brand, and his focus on having a professional, highly trained, skilled workforce.

Graham then opened up a world of hands-on discovery and exploration by inviting us to embark on a tour through the front-of-house and back-office operations of the hotel. We were able to see the mesmerizing atrium, the stunning restaurant with panoramic views of the city skyline, the fancy guest suites, the lavish cocktail lounge, and the kitchen, a hive of activity. The air was filled with pleasant aromas and the sounds of pots and pans clanging as the team of sixty chefs prepared for the evening diners. Remember: the environment and the atmosphere in which one works is also very important to their tenure at a company, or hotel in this case.

I was impressed by what I saw and became determined to land a job at this hotel. After the event, I prepared day and night for the series of interviews, practicing mock interviews with my father and a family friend. I was over the moon when I received an offer to become an apprentice chef. It was a surreal feeling, and I couldn't wait to start my journey at the hotel. The hiring event at the Regent Hotel was a life-changing experience. It allowed me to understand the brand, the vision, and the exciting, fast-paced environment in which I would potentially be working.

In my journey as an employer, I've learned not to get sidetracked by the allure of new tech tools and platforms and to always remember the value of the tried-and-true traditional hiring methods. Involving family members (minors may need parental consent to work, in any case) in the process by organizing an expo, career fair, career night, or open house can be a nice touch. This may seem old-fashioned, but it can open a valuable perspective and provide a support system for young adults entering the workforce.

Attending a hiring event at the workplace and/or touring the facility allows potential employees to experience what it would be like to work in that business or industry. It provides an opportunity to establish a human connection with potential employees. It sets a foundation for a stronger, more fulfilling work relationship. Embracing the classics can add a touch of humanity, which is frequently lost in a world where technology so often dominates.

Revolutionizing the hiring process

As a hiring manager, you know that the traditional hiring process can be limiting, leading to missed opportunities and a lack of diversity in the workplace. That's why it's important to reframe the hiring process to help you find the best candidates for your organization. Here are some key themes and issues to keep in mind as you work to improve your hiring process.

Team involvement

Your team knows your organization best and can help you identify the right candidate for the job. Involve your team in the hiring process, from reviewing resumes to conducting interviews. This can help ensure that the candidate you choose is the right fit for your organization's culture and values. You can also reward team members for recommending quality candidates. Referrals are one of the most effective ways for companies to find quality candidates. Having employees recommend talents individuals is a plus because they already know the position and the culture of the workplace, as well as the candidate. In my experience, involving the team not only empowers them but often leads to discovering candidates who might have otherwise been overlooked. And team members can also provide details about working in a specific group setting that even managers may forget to address. It's a practice that has enriched our company culture and brought in diverse talents who truly align with our values.

Revolutionizing the hiring process can be a challenge, but it's worth the effort. By focusing on diversity and inclusion, a mix of both technical and personal skills, candidate experience, technology, and team involvement, you can find the best candidates for your organization and build a diverse and talented workforce. Embarking on this journey to revolutionize your hiring process is more than just a strategic move; it's a commitment to nurturing a workplace where diversity, skill, and innovation thrive. It's time to turn these insights into action and watch your organization transform.

The human element in hiring

Let's take a moment to look at applicant tracking systems (ATS). To me, they are the frozen microwave TV dinners of the hiring world: quick and convenient, but that's about it. Let's be real: they're nothing like a good homemade meal. Last time I checked a TV dinner, it listed all these mystery ingredients (not in a good way): monosodium glutamate (MSG—yuck), carrageenan, disodium inosinate (another yuck), xanthan gum, sodium benzoate E211 (can turn into a carcinogen, no thanks), and those infamous colorants, Red 40 and Yellow 5. *What's in this package I'm about to microwave and eat? Is it food or a science experiment?*

The same skepticism applies to ATS. These systems, often a black box to the companies that use them, can overlook key candidate qualities because of their narrow programming focus. The risk? You are likely missing out on exceptional talent because they don't fit an algorithm.

Here's the irony: the internet is swamped with more tips on tricking ATS than actual information about these systems themselves. Seems counterproductive, right? If you lose one great candidate, it's not just a missed opportunity; it's a costly mistake. That's why I believe in treating great candidates like gold.

ATS often fail to capture the essence of what makes a candidate stand out—their personal skills and experiences. If you are using an ATS, consider shifting back to a more human-centric recruitment approach, in which unique qualities and potential are valued over fitting into a predefined algorithm.

The flaws in ATS are glaring, from rejecting candidates over trivial formatting issues to increasing the ease of gaming the system. What's clear to me with ATS is that it's become a case of technology outsmarting technology.

If you have your doubts, here's a case in point.

I asked an AI content generator, "Can you help me write an ATS-friendly resume that will get past the algorithms and get me an interview?"

And here's the response I received: "Of course, I can help you create an ATS-friendly resume that increases your chances of getting past the algorithms and securing an interview. Below is a step-by-step guide and a sample resume template to achieve this."

My takeaway from this short interaction was that the best policy is to simply keep it simple and human. Stay away from ATS, TV dinners, and asking AI to do your homework for you! Don't get me wrong: AI can be a beneficial tool, but use it to help you in a manner that's ethical and straightforward.

The employment solution that's right under your nose

Here's one sure way of securing good talent: tap into the talent you already have. Invest in the talent that already exists within the company. Investing in on-the-job training and upskilling for current employees can provide numerous benefits and ensure the future success of a business. Although both on-the-job training and upskilling are geared towards enhancing employee skills, they serve distinct purposes. Training improves an employee's potential at a current position whereas upskilling aims to equip employees with new skills and knowledge to prepare them for future challenges and roles within the company. It also minimizes turnover, which saves you money. And it lets people see a path in front of them to follow, which increases their motivation and desire to stay with the company. Employees also see that you appreciate them, which is more significant than it sounds. In the quest for employee retention, entrepreneurs need to brace for typical roadblocks—think poor management communication, mundane tasks, or scant career progression opportunities. Creating an environment that encourages two-way dialogue between employees and managers, along with clear standards and rewarding incentives, are excellent strategies to boost morale in the workplace. With these measures in place, businesses can ensure that their team remains motivated and devoted long term.

Navigating the tricky terrain of employee retention, I've learned that genuine dialogue and clear pathways for growth are not just strategies but the lifelines of a thriving work culture. Reflecting on my journey, I realize that the moments we took to genuinely listen and provide clear growth opportunities didn't just reduce turnover; they transformed our workplace into a dynamic environment where everyone's potential was recognized and nurtured.

Investing in your employees is an important part of cultivating a successful team. Listen to employee feedback, engage with them on relevant topics, provide incentives and rewards, and ensure they feel supported by their team members. These efforts will drive motivation and retention rates.

Attracting new talent

In my experience, attracting top talent solely through job postings on major platforms can be a struggle. To attract creative minds, you must innovate beyond the traditional in your hiring outreach. The quest for exceptional talent demands strategies as inventive as the individuals you're aiming to recruit.

Consider these innovative hiring strategies to attract external talent:

- Tap into local recruitment networks to build referrals and spread awareness of current vacancies.

- Host industry-related events that double as recruitment events. This is a great way to engage with potential employees while they gain valuable insight on what it's like to work in that field. They can even be virtual events or interactive webinars. These events provide an excellent opportunity for potential hires to directly engage with team leaders and ask questions.

- Enhance your company as a place to build a career. Incorporate interactive elements like virtual office tours and employee testimonial videos to provide insights into your company's mission, values, and culture.

- Leverage social media platforms such as LinkedIn, X, Instagram, and Facebook to showcase your company culture and broadcast job openings. Engaging (authentically) with your audience on these platforms can significantly widen your reach.

- Utilize niche job boards to reach the specific talent you're searching for. For example, Stack Overflow is ideal for tech roles while Medzilla caters to healthcare. There are similar niche boards for various other industries, offering targeted talent pools.

- Connect with educational design programs, as well as clubs or associations. This will also help get word out about open positions.

- Remember the human factor: invest in meaningful conversations, and you may be surprised at how far those connections can take you.

You can also consider implementing an employee referral program. I've found success in refer-a-friend programs, in which employees are rewarded for their referrals. I see this as a case of like attracts like—a great employee is likely to refer someone equally talented. After all, why would a top performer refer someone they know is not a suitable candidate or whose qualities they do not respect?

Additionally, offering internships and apprenticeships, participating in career fairs, connecting with educators for a talent pipeline, and promoting your environmental commitments can also significantly enhance your talent acquisition efforts.

If you already have some strategies in place, you should promote them regularly to make it clear that your company can overcome talent shortages while also fostering a dynamic and forward-thinking work environment.

Industry events and more

If you want to find the perfect employee for your business, look no further than industry events and recruitment networks. Engaging with people on a personal level is so important; having potential employees meet current members of staff can help them gain insight into the role for which they are applying. Also, consider local referral circles between businesses, which can help your job postings get greater visibility. The point is don't just focus on the obvious methods such as advertising online. Looking for an unconventional way to stand out against your competition in the European job market? From scuba diving interviews in Poland to private concerts and jazz music showcases in Austria or Italy's unique open forums held around food themes— these and other "crazy" ideas have seen success.

You might also talk to your vendors because they know people in your industry, and perhaps they know of talent looking to change jobs. It can't hurt. You could also reach out directly to your customers. In IKEA Australia, for instance, job ads were included in each shipment of furniture they made to IKEA customers.

How about holding a contest? People love competitions. MGM in Vegas found a head chef though a cooking contest. When LEGO was looking for new people, they held a LEGO building contest. Even Broadway held a televised contest to find the next lead in *Legally Blonde* when the original star of the show, Laura Bell Bundy, left.

To find the ideal candidate for your next role, think beyond traditional recruitment strategies. Targeting potential candidates directly can be very effective, in addition to casting a wide net. Hosting hiring events and inviting parents or family members of prospects is an excellent way to gain important insight into their background—plus, it's particularly useful when recruiting younger generations.

And speaking of younger generations, posting on job boards at colleges, high schools, and tech schools is great, but you can also drill down and post jobs for chefs at culinary institutes, nurses at nursing schools, and so forth—you get the idea. To take it one step further, post ads (with permission, of course) at popular student hangout spots. For example, if they all go to a local diner after classes end for the day, have a job ad on the diner menus; it can be very inexpensive and effective advertising.

And speaking of ads, they are a communication tool geared for getting the right people into your company. Yet it still amazes me how many mundane ads I see out there, particularly when companies are trying to connect with the next generation of workers. Some of this content is as vanilla as ice cream. I recently saw an advertisement for HVAC apprentice:

"Employer seeks hardworking individual to fill the position. The successful candidate must possess a willingness to learn and a desire to pursue a career in the electrical field. You must have the ability to follow directions, display attention to detail, and be punctual."

No offense to the company or their copywriters, but they have a snowflake's chance in hell of finding a great candidate, so I rewrote the ad:

"Grab hold of your future. Earn while you learn—get paid from day one. Build on-the-job experience with an industry-leading organization. We're all about training and growth, so show us your passion, eye for detail, and reliability while we support you with mentorship and career guidance. Take control of your destiny and #ElectrifyYourCareer today!"

I left out phrases like "follow directions" and "be punctual," which should be implied in order to get any job. My suggested rewrite underscores the importance of connecting to people's interests and needs. Words like "earn," "learn," "training," and "growth" all fit the bill.

To captivate your target audience, it's crucial to tune into their frequencies—understand their motivations and create a connection to your company that goes beyond the job description. It's about lighting a fire under their ambitions and turning the knob to success.

CHAPTER 14

Remote Work

———

GONE ARE THE DAYS WHEN THE OFFICE WAS JUST THE office. Enter COVID-19, reshaping our workspaces overnight. This wasn't just a temporary fix; it was the start of a revolution in how we work.

In 2020, we saw a massive shift to remote work—a necessity turned into a global experiment in workplace flexibility. It also sent commercial real estate into a global nosedive. And yet most thriving businesses are still thriving as usual.

While I was contemplating the evolution of our workspaces, the CBS news program *60 Minutes* did a segment which grabbed my attention. Imagine this: more than 95 million square feet of office space in New York City, equivalent to thirty Empire State Buildings, sits unoccupied. As we embrace the convenience of remote work, these towering symbols of corporate America are quietly turning into ghost towers. It's a sobering reminder that the ripple effects of our workspace choices extend far beyond the confines of our home offices.

The shift is seismic, reshaping not just the skyline but the very fabric of our cities. As Stijn Van Nieuwerburgh of Columbia Business

School insightfully remarked, there's a "fundamental uncertainty we face about the future of work arrangements," hinting at the profound societal and economic transformations just beginning to unfold. [1]

Van Nieuwerburgh described this as the "urban doom loop." He warned that declining office values and a shrinking tax base could significantly impact urban economies. This concept highlights the urgent need for innovative urban planning and adaptation in response to the changing work landscape.

And yet remote work is not for everyone. First, not every job can shift to a home office. Firefighters, surgeons, manufacturing workers, and even restaurant staffs have roles that demand a physical presence. In other cases, people work better, more creatively and collaboratively, when they are around others.

And then there's the hybrid model, in which employees work some days in the office and some days remote. The numbers from a recent Gallup poll[2] indicate a significant move towards this hybrid model. In 2023, just 20 percent of remote-capable employees were working full-time on site, a significant decrease from 60 percent in 2019. Put another way, 80 percent of remote-capable employees in 2023 were able to take advantage of that capability to work off-site at least some of the time. Meanwhile, full-time remote workers increased from 8 to 10 percent. This demonstrates a dramatic shift from traditional office settings to more flexible arrangements, with hybrid work rapidly becoming the dominant work style among remote-capable employees.

Are there downsides? Of course. Work–life balance has become an uncomfortable tightrope walk. The home, once a sanctuary, is now an office, changing the dynamics of work and life. Distractions abound, and the isolation can be suffocating. It's not just about missing office chit-chat; it's about losing vital human contact.

While delving into the cons of remote work, let's reflect on a legal case that caught my attention. It involved an eighteen-year employee and his company, embroiled in a dispute over remote work monitoring. The crux? The company's use of sophisticated tracking technology to monitor the employee's every digital move, such as keystrokes, raising questions about privacy and trust in remote work setups.

Drawing insights from a BBC article titled "How Worker Surveillance Is Backfiring on Employers," we see this isn't an isolated incident. The article sheds light on the broader implications of such surveillance practices. It reveals how, in a bid to ensure productivity, companies are resorting to measures that can inadvertently foster a culture of distrust and anxiety. Karen Levy, an associate professor at Cornell University, points out the pitfalls of excessive monitoring, noting its potential to increase stress, prompt employee turnover, and even lead to deliberate underperformance.[3]

So how do you maintain productivity and team cohesion in a remote workplace? Video software might be embracing hybrid models, but for many businesses, the challenge is keeping the team spirit alive while driving productivity.

It's been reported by CNBC, based on numbers from an outside survey of 1,000 US company leaders, that "a whopping 90 percent of companies plan to implement return-to-office policies by the end of 2024 and nearly 30 percent say their company will threaten to fire employees who don't comply with in-office requirements."[4] However, it has also been reported by PR Newswire that an "Integrated Benefits Institute Analysis indicates that 47 percent of US employees say they'll quit if their employer orders them to return to the office full time."[5]

Perhaps a hybrid solution will be the compromise?

Developing a hybrid work strategy

Hybrid workplaces have come into vogue for a variety of reasons, including less traffic (meaning a lower carbon footprint) and happier employees who get to spend more time with their families.

For a successful hybrid work strategy, start with a robust, long-term plan, emphasizing a leadership commitment to both the success of the business and the contributions made by the employees. Both sides need to be able to focus on a strategy that benefits everyone involved.

Your strategy should then integrate the various elements we've discussed throughout this book. Tailor it to your company's unique culture, with a focus on fostering collaboration and considering the specific needs of your team. When prioritizing in-office work, aim for a workspace that's both inviting and functional. You also need to keep your technology and training methods up-to-date to support a flexible work environment. The key here is thoughtfulness. When it pertains to a remote setup, employees need to be able to focus without distractions while working. If both sides remain honest and diligent and keep the lines of communication open, the hybrid solution can remain beneficial to everyone involved, as well as the business.

Your strategy as a manager, owner, or leader should combine various aspects like office design, technology, performance management, and training in a manner that aligns with your company's specific requirements and culture. The significant reasons for being in the office environment and the significant reasons for working remotely should both be discussed, with the pros of each side clearly explained. You must account for both sides without hurting the production or output of the company in any way. Many hybrid companies are highly successful, and it can be the best of both worlds if done correctly.

Among the most successful hybrid companies are Adobe, Allstate, Amazon, Brighthouse Financial, Cisco, Citigroup, Coleman Research, DoorDash, Google, Gravity Payments, Hachette Book Group, Meta (Facebook), Microsoft, Salesforce, Slack, Unilever, and UnitedHealth Group, to name a few. If they can do it, so can your company.

CHAPTER 15

Designing Inspirational Workspaces

———

THE TIMES, THEY ARE A-CHANGIN', AND THE OFFICE IS NO exception. It's not just a boring, beige cubicle anymore; people want to be excited to go to work, to feel like they're part of something special. But how do you make that happen? It's all about creating a space as unique and interesting as the people who work there. You want your office to be more than just functional; you want it to be a destination your team is pumped up to visit.

You've probably heard of companies (strangely always tech or financial startups) trying too hard with table tennis, foosball tables, climbing walls, and people running around with Nerf guns. But it's not supposed to be a play center. It's about finding that balance—making your space an engaging, uplifting, cheerful, yet professional environment.

This is where things get interesting. Employers are starting to realize that they must invest in their workspaces if they want to keep their top talent. I'm talking about creating an environment that feels like a community in which everyone is connected.

It's about sculpting a space that resonates, transcending the typical workspace to echo the cozy, nurturing vibe of a home office. Companies that put effort into their office environment can create a place that's both practical and inspiring—a place that makes employees feel like they're part of something special.

If you design a space full of personality and charisma that excites people to get out of bed in the morning and show up, you'll be rewarded with a motivated, engaged workforce that's ready to take on whatever the world throws their way. If the environment and design reeks of 1977, complete with grey cubical walls and sad disco balls, people may not want to show up at all.

I have created a dynamic yet flexible environment, yet I still have workstations. Most are hot desks, meaning you don't have to sit at the same desk every day. However, since many people enjoy having "their own spot" in which they feel comfortable, that can also be arranged. I also created a nook in what was an old storeroom—we added a built-in table and bench seats (like those old-school built-in family kitchen tables) and installed some cool library book wallpaper and an architectural light. Now it's a popular place for small meetings or solo work.

Then there are some tried-and-true design features you may consider for an office environment, such as large colorful paintings, particularly from local artists (I like paintings by Indigenous artists), plants or plant walls (real or fake), big chairs, a comfy couch, separate areas for work and relaxation, unusual clocks, area rugs, and of course bold colors that brighten up the space. I also like wallpaper not unlike some of those Zoom backgrounds. It's also advantageous not to crowd the room. Open spaces indicate more freedom.

There are tons of photos of modern workspaces found online. You can always assemble a group of employees to brainstorm. Let people have a hand in the design of their own workspaces.

Another dimension to consider in workspace design is the great outdoors. Let's think outside the four walls of the traditional office setting. Consider using outdoor spaces in your community, like parks, beaches, and trails, for team interactions and activities. It's completely free—no need to spend on renting equipment or booking venues. Take advantage of the natural resources and beauty of your community to promote teamwork and creativity. Providing your team with a unique and refreshing experience breaks the monotony of traditional office work. This approach not only fosters a sense of community and well-being among employees but also encourages creative thinking in a more relaxed and open environment.

Although it is true that not everyone works in a traditional office, there is usually some space in which people congregate. Factories, retail locations, restaurants, police stations, hotels, and even hospitals—none of these are designed as primarily office spaces, but they do have offices within. And although you may not have a large communal area, you can allow people to have some freedom to design their own offices. Even if it's a few photos and a painting and a comfy chair or two, encourage people to have a say in their daily destination.

The four-day workweek

What would Dolly Parton have to sing about if everyone starts working a four-day workweek? Perhaps she would need to write a sequel to her smash hit song "9 to 5" and call it "4, Living More." In all seriousness, the four-day workweek is a concept that could bring about significant changes to our lifestyles. While there are pros and cons, it's essential to approach the topic with an open mind and consider the potential impact on individuals and society.

The essence of the four-day workweek means doing the same amount of work in fewer hours or extending the workday slightly to compensate for an extra day off each week. Pay typically remains the same, but that may not be the case in all companies. While the four-day workweek offers notable advantages for both employers and employees, it can also have its drawbacks. It's crucial to weigh these benefits against possible drawbacks before making a shift. The crucial question from the business side is this: will we get the same production? If the answer is yes, you may be en route to a four-day workweek.

In many cases, employees are happier working four days and have been shown to produce better results even with fewer hours. The employees welcomed the trade-off of a few longer days for a third day off each week.

Golden Police Department in Colorado piloted a four-day workweek starting in mid 2023. The department embarked on a program named The Best for Golden, shifting all employees (which included all fifty-plus police officers and around twenty-eight administrative staff) to a thirty-two-hour workweek without reducing their pay. This initiative aimed to address the high burnout rates and turnover often seen in law enforcement. By offering a shorter workweek, they hoped to enhance employee well-being and efficiency, potentially setting a new standard in policing. Metrics are being monitored closely to ensure that service quality remained high. Some early results indicated a reduction in overtime costs, an uptick in retention, and an overall increase in employee satisfaction. The success of this pilot could serve as a blueprint for similar changes across other city departments, potentially redefining work–life balance in demanding professions like law enforcement. Watch this space.

Pros:

- **Boosted productivity:** Studies worldwide reveal employees are often more productive with fewer work hours. Shifting from counting hours to measuring results can ramp up efficiency and your bottom line. The majority of companies testing a four-day week did not want to go back.

- **Enhanced employee well-being:** A shorter workweek means happier, healthier employees less likely to jump ship. This shift can significantly cut down on turnover, fostering a stable and engaged workforce.

- **Environmental gains:** Fewer commuting days mean a smaller carbon footprint, contributing to environmental sustainability.

- Family time can increase with an extra day off each week.

Cons:

- **Operational hurdles:** Not all industries can swing a four-day schedule without hiccups. Challenges include adjusting contracts, managing holiday entitlements, and ensuring service continuity—especially if your business operates five days a week, as is typically the case.

- **Adaptation struggles:** The transition may not suit everyone. Some employees might find the longer workdays a tough trade-off for an extra day off, requiring support to adjust. Others may have family obligations that make it difficult to work longer hours.

Considering a four-day workweek? Start with the facts, listen to your team, and maybe dip your toes in with a pilot program. It's about finding balance in the new age of work, not just following a trend.

Leave us alone!

Whether you're working four or five days a week, you are entitled to time off, which means no work, not even having to respond to your boss or colleagues if you so choose—and you should. In fact, in Australia, the senate passed what they've called "right to disconnect" legislation. What this means is that your supervisors cannot legally contact you in any way, shape, or form during your time off—no emails, no texts, no calls, no visits, and one would guess if they send a carrier pigeon, you can just shoo it away. Spain, France, Portugal, and Columbia are among other nations that have similar laws. While intended to support balance, policies like this may not suit every industry equally and clearly need flexibility to be effective.

Custom learning spaces

In the late twentieth and early twenty-first century, initiatives like the Crotonville Leadership Center in New York emerged. These centers are seen as investments in employees, offering opportunities for learning, growth, and skill development.

The creation of these leadership and training centers demonstrates a company's commitment to their employees and their desire to provide them with the resources and support needed to succeed.

BHP, a major player in the mining industry with a massive 80,000-strong workforce, embarked on an ambitious project at the turn of the millennium. The company aimed to build a world-class training center for its executives and senior managers. The HR department led the charge, convincing the CEO and board to invest $50 million in a state-of-the-art facility with a conference center, corporate university, and luxurious hotel elements. The building, an architectural masterpiece, featured curved roofs, 150,000 square feet of interlinked buildings, and a golf course surrounded by rolling hills.

Executives were used to attending training and conferences at resort destinations like Hawaii and Las Vegas. The news that the facility would be managed through the HR division rather than a hotel operator, the idea of employees sleeping under the company's roof, was not well received. Despite its impressive design and facilities, the training center failed to reach its potential.

Upon BHP Billiton appointing as its new CEO Brian Gilbertson, known for his ambitious leadership style, the company braced for a cultural shift. Gilbertson's grandiose entrances by helicopter in Johannesburg, wryly reported by employees as "the ego has landed," heralded a new era. The start of his tenure was marked by a swift, decisive action: divesting from the Global Leadership Centre just a few months into his role. This move, influenced by factors such as the company's evolving workforce, escalating travel costs, and the rise of online conferencing, suggested a strategic realignment with the company's broader objectives. Although opinions may vary, it appeared that Gilbertson's decision was aligned with the long-term interests of the business.

Nevertheless, it's important to consider all aspects of the business and make decisions that closely align with the goals and vision of the company.

Advancements in remote communication have made it easier than ever to talk with people in all corners of the world, face to face and with little effort. This minimizes the need for significant business travel, which cuts expenses and decreases your business's carbon footprint. However, although attending gatherings in the company's

state-of-the-art brick-and-mortar facilities is nice, there are alterna-
tives. Owning a training facility presents challenges, particularly given
economic fluctuations and varying company fortunes. While BHP's
initiative focused exclusively on the leadership development and training of its employees, a more dual-purpose approach—one that also
actively engages customers and partners—might have better served
the center's longevity and utility.

And that's precisely what DHL, a giant in global logistics, has done.
DHL operates four major Innovation Centers worldwide, located
in Germany, Singapore, Dubai, and Chicago. Each center is fully
operational, actively showcasing the latest advancements in logistics technology. The Chicago facility was opened in 2019 and is an incredible site
to visit. They welcome tours, which you can request on their website.
Imagine a world where transportation infrastructure is transformed by
advancements in robotics and automation, AI, self-driving vehicles, and
VR. This 24,000-square-foot facility is a state-of-the-art marvel featuring high-tech amenities, futuristic designs, an awe-inspiring foyer, and
abundant meeting spaces. With the ability to host trend and innovation
events for up to three hundred guests, DHL's innovation center is a hub
for inspiration, connection, and engagement.

Coworking spaces

Coworking spaces represent another shift in how we approach work,
from a solitary and isolated activity to a collaborative and communi-
ty-based endeavor. But like all things in life, there are pros and cons
to this new way of working, and we must navigate them carefully to
reap the benefits.

Coworking spaces are great for freelancers who crave human interaction and community. They offer an environment conducive to productivity and creativity, with opportunities to network and collaborate with like-minded individuals. Coworking spaces provide a much-needed solution in a world where loneliness and isolation are a big issue.

However, the downsides of coworking spaces cannot be ignored. For some workers, the noise and distraction can be overwhelming, hindering their ability to focus and be productive. And let's not forget the high cost of renting a desk or private office, which can be a significant barrier for those on a slim budget or in costly cities.

I have spent time in many coworking spaces in the last few years and found they're like the Swiss Army knife of the modern professional: they've got a tool for every job. It's all fun and games until someone answers their phone in the silent zone.

The answer lies in providing a supportive and flexible workspace that targets the needs of its members. Coworking spaces must be clean and well lit, offer designated quiet zones for workers who need a peaceful environment to focus, and provide flexible pricing plans to accommodate different budgets. Moreover, the design of the workspace itself can make a massive difference in productivity and community building.

Coworking environments incorporating open spaces, comfortable furniture, and natural lighting can create an atmosphere that promotes collaboration and creativity. And let's not forget the importance of networking and educational events, encouraging members to share their expertise and connect with others. Of course there need to be some guidelines with which everyone needs to comply. In other words, if everyone works and plays by the rules, these can be marvelous places to get your work done.

Work and learn spaces

The atmosphere of your workspace matters. You know when you step into a well-designed workspace where someone has taken care and given attention to the simple things: the color of the walls, the use of natural or other light, the ambiance . . . It's a place that invites you in and beckons you to stay (and yes—work).

Visiting Google's New York offices, located above the lively Chelsea Market, I couldn't help but soak in this ambiance. It was more than just the employees zipping from one part of the space to another on scooters to meet me. Yet somewhere in the back of my mind, I half-expected to see a hoverboard glide past—sadly, not. The place had energy, making the typical office vibe seem a world away. Every corner of Google's office boasted colorful murals and an eclectic mix of workspaces, inviting employees to collaborate. And yes, those funky little nooks and crannies at Google were everywhere, though I had to wonder if some favored style over comfort. All in all, hats off to Google. They certainly nailed this office space in the heart of Manhattan.

But can cool workplaces exist outside of traditional offices? Let's look at the McLaren factory in the United Kingdom, a true masterpiece in workplace design. This sleek, futuristic, exceptional facility was meticulously crafted by the visionary architect Lord Norman Foster, the brilliant mind behind iconic structures such as the London Gherkin, an energy-efficient skyscraper that looks like a giant pickle (hence the nickname).

What set the design brief for this factory apart was the aspiration to create a space where every person who walked through its doors felt an unrelenting desire to strive for excellence. The McLaren factory was not just about assembling Formula 1 race cars; it was about cultivating an environment where the pursuit of perfection becomes a way of life.

Every corner of the building was meticulously planned to inspire and motivate. Every detail echoed a commitment to precision and innovation, from the pristine assembly lines, where cutting-edge technology meets the skilled hands of craftsmen, to the breakout areas designed for brainstorming and collaboration. It was not unlike the Porsche factory I discussed in Chapter 8.

In this extraordinary setting, employees weren't just workers but artisans crafting machines built for speed and performance. The design of the McLaren factory itself was a testament to the philosophy that every fraction of a second counted in Formula 1 racing. It was a place where excellence was not just a goal but a daily reality and where every individual was empowered to contribute to the legacy of speed, precision, and success.

If your company's goal is to get employees back to an office or workplace, full-time or part-time, consider the stick or carrot analogy. You can force them with compulsion and directives (and with threats, as some companies did, to return or be fired). Or you can take a different route: create a space to which your people actually wish to return.

Don't rule out grunge and graffiti

Looking to create a workspace that's both visually engaging and energizing? Incorporating grunge and industrial design elements along with bold graffiti art can make a unique and inspiring environment that captures the spirit of urban life. Originating in the SoHo neighborhood of New York City in the 1960s and 1970s, the industrial look has become a popular and edgy design trend. By incorporating raw, exposed materials like concrete floors, brick walls, and metal pipes, you can create an unconventional and visually engaging workspace that captures the gritty, edgy spirit of industrial drive. In addition to its distinctive aesthetic, the grunge and industrial look also offers eco-friendly benefits. You can promote sustainability and reduce your environmental impact by incorporating elements like a green wall, energy-efficient lighting, and repurposed items. This may not fit all locations, but it definitely draws attention, supports the environment, makes for a fun place to work—and yes, inspires employees.

Canary in the coal mine

Just to set the record straight for any canary liberationists out there, the canary I'm talking about isn't a feathered friend, nor were any canaries harmed in the making of this book; it's simply a metaphor.

I'm in the heart of a buzzing D.C. café, as a colleague quipped about the "Giant Sucking Sound"—his colorful term for the mass talent exodus known as the Great Resignation triggered by the COVID-19 pandemic. The pandemic laid bare a crisis in employee satisfaction, with a flood of talent departing their roles, not just in search of a different job but seeking a more meaningful existence, sometimes stepping away from the workforce entirely. There were many questions about what was driving this trend and whether it was just a passing fad or a result of larger underlying issues in the workforce.

What was really happening here? It was a statement to employers. I've spoken to countless individuals who were not just seeking another job but a role that offered them a sense of fulfillment and recognition. They were driven by factors such as job dissatisfaction, a desire to pursue their passions, better leadership, and a need to be provided with more than just a paycheck. I remember feeling a mix of surprise and understanding when the Great Resignation first made headlines. It echoed the personal conversations I've had with many professionals, each expressing a deep yearning for something more fulfilling than the status quo.

Despite this shift in the job market, it's important to focus on creating a positive and motivating work environment that keep employees satisfied and engaged. After all, as the classic country song "Take This Job and Shove It" reminds us, job dissatisfaction has been a common theme for decades. The term "the Great Dissatisfaction" seems to hit closer to home. It encapsulates the collective sentiment I've encountered in my career: a quest for recognition and purpose, a work life that echoes one's values and even pays the bills.

Interestingly, amidst this wave of change, there was an unseen outcome: many who rode the wave of the Great Resignation are now wondering if that was, in fact, a good move. In the wake of this shift, a surprising trend has emerged: a number of individuals who made the leap during the Great Resignation are now experiencing "the Great Regret" as they reassess their impulsive decisions against the backdrop of financial responsibilities and evolving job markets.

Although the Great Resignation benefitted some and put others in challenging situations, it succeeded at opening the eyes of many in management and leadership who realized that too many employees were not happy with the status quo. They realized that things had to change, as we've discussed all through this book.

CHAPTER 16

Pioneering Recruitment Strategies

———

JOB HOPPING? UNHEARD OF IN WALTER ORTHMANN'S DAY.
Walter started working at a textile company at fifteen and didn't stop until eighty-four years later—yes, you read that right, eighty-four years! That belongs in the Guinness World Records, if it's not already there. Orthmann's story isn't just a record-breaking marvel; it's a window into a bygone era when lifelong tenure at one job was common. You might even know of a person who spent their whole career at the same company, but chances are that was decades ago. Now, let's contrast that with today's dynamic job market.

Job hopping is the common phrase for employees frequently changing positions within a relatively short period. Is this a bad thing? In the past, absolutely. Leaving a job was a sign of disloyalty. Today it depends on who's doing the hopping and why.

What can statistics tell us? The Bureau of Labor Statistics reveals some notable numbers. For example, Americans born in the early 1980s hold an average of nine jobs from ages eighteen to thirty-six; those born from 1957 to 1964 held almost thirteen jobs from ages eighteen to fifty-six.[1] Another recent statistic shows that workers are now changing jobs every four years, while a Zippia survey found that the average Millennial sticks around for an average of only 2.75 years.[2] This pattern shows a drastic increase in job mobility, marking the clear departure from past job tenure trends. Meanwhile, another study from UKG found that 43 percent of individuals who left their jobs during the pandemic realized they were better off in their old job.[3] So let's understand why people are shifting jobs so frequently.

First, money. Yes, higher pay is a big motivator. If another company offers a significant salary jump, it's a no-brainer for many. However, many people want to expand their horizons, not just their wallets. They're after new experiences, skills, and roles in which they have a better chance to grow, reach higher levels, and embrace learning opportunities that matter. Others are job hopping to improve their work–life balance.

This phenomenon should also present an opportunity for employers. In my own company, I have worked closely with our recruitment team to reframe how we view candidates with a "chop and change" work history. We're keenly aware that fresh perspectives and diverse skill sets are invaluable, particularly from younger employees. Many of the candidates may not have extensive work experience, but we look for indicators of commitment and follow-through, like sticking with a sports season or completing projects they started. It's about recognizing potential and nurturing it, regardless of a candidate's job-hopping history.

In my former industry, the hospitality sector, senior chefs and hotel managers hop from one prestigious hotel to another, one country to another, often in the same hotel chain, but it's accepted that these individuals come and go through many workplaces in their careers. In fact, it's expected that you move around. If you stay in one place too long, you may be seen as food that's been around awhile—potentially stale. For me, job hopping throughout Europe gave me an unparalleled culinary education as I learned about a wide range of cuisines unlike that of my homeland, Australia, with its shrimp on the barbie, pie, and sauce culinary reputation.

Can you (or should you) calm a job hopper?

What can recruiters do when they find a job hopper? I would start looking for clear indicators of their potential. Look for those who have used each role to build their skill set and can show how these skills translate to your needs. But watch out for candidates who can't clearly articulate why they've moved around. Look for those who have strategically job hopped for career growth, skill development, and to be challenged rather than because they were bored. Also, remember that some job hoppers, at least in the United States, should be given a little slack—three recessions in less than twenty-five years often mean that the company they worked for was laying people off or went out of business. Hence they had no choice but to find another job.

In essence, understanding and adapting to this job hopping trend aren't just about retention; it's about creating an environment where talent wants to grow, thrive, and maybe, just maybe, decide to stay.

In humans we trust

Trusting in humanity aligns with the evolving understanding of fair compensation. In a world where living wages become the norm, we uplift the very essence of our workforce, allowing creativity and empathy to flourish without the burden of financial stress.

While robotics and AI continue their march forward, they falter at the frontier of humanity—our realm of creativity, empathy, and nuanced judgment. It's this profoundly human skill set that remains our unmatched strength. Now, more than ever, we need people who bring creativity and empathy to our tech-heavy workplaces.

By valuing candidates brimming with creativity and innovation, you're not just filling a role; you're inviting a breath of fresh, unconventional ideas that keep your organization at the forefront of the game. Creative thinkers can also offer clever advertisements, unusual marketing concepts, new sales and innovative strategies, and inspiring team-building activities.

Walt Disney believed that the best companies were those that empowered their employees. He famously said, "You can design and create and build the most wonderful place in the world, but it takes people to make the dream a reality." Disney's emphasis on employee empowerment and training has been a major factor in the company's amazing success over the years. It's not just about creating a magical environment; it's also about having knowledgeable and enthusiastic employees who can enhance the customer experience.

Don't forget problem-solving. This is a skill that robots and machines don't possess, at least not yet. Candidates who excel at problem-solving can help your organization identify and address complex problems, develop innovative solutions, and keep your business running smoothly.

Undoubtedly, digital literacy is not just a skill but a necessity now. Seek out candidates who don't just understand the latest tech but converse fluently with it, staying a step ahead of the ever-evolving digital curve.

Last but not least, we have collaboration. By championing collaboration and sculpting workplaces where human ingenuity meets machine precision, we don't just achieve; we redefine what's possible. It's the human touch that shines as our most priceless asset, steering our interactions with sincerity and warmth that no technology can replicate.

Creating a great candidate experience

If you want to sell people a new product, you want to create something that will draw their attention and meet their needs. To do this, you want to create a great customer experience. Likewise, you want to create a great candidate experience if you are going to sell a candidate on why they should work for you.

We've talked about many of the ingredients that should be baked into a great candidate experience. Personalization is a huge plus. While you expect that candidates will familiarize themselves with your business, it's also paramount that you take the time to learn about them. Tailor your interactions to address each candidate's specific needs and preferences, demonstrating your commitment to their individual journey and serving as an icebreaker for nervous candidates. Invest time in understanding each candidate, showing that you respect and value their efforts.

And if you really want to set yourself apart, leverage your entrepreneurial creativity to devise innovative approaches that excite candidates about working with you:

- **Stay connected throughout the hiring process:** Ensure consistent communication via email after the interview to keep candidates informed and engaged on what your company is doing, and provide regular updates on the status of their application. This will keep them engaged and show that you value their time and effort.

- **Be open, transparent, and honest:** Don't sugarcoat the job, make false promises, or use trendy jargon just to get a candidate through the door. Be honest about the position, the company culture, and the expectations of the role. This will help ensure a good fit and build trust with candidates while letting them know early on that this might or might not be a good fit. Always be professional, and never say never—you have no idea what new jobs will potentially arise in your company.

- **Show appreciation and gratitude:** Don't forget to thank candidates for their time and effort, even if they don't get the job. A straightforward thank-you note or email can significantly contribute to a positive candidate experience, fostering lasting connections.

The cup-of-joe test

It's the seemingly minor actions that often speak the loudest. Here you are, a candidate at a job interview, but this is not your run-of-the-mill, sit-across-the-desk arrangement. You're met in the reception area by tech and recruitment CEO Trent Innes, who takes you through to the office kitchen. You sit down. He offers and makes you a tea or coffee. The more informal interview flows, but the real "Trent test" is brewing silently. What happens to that empty cup once the interview wraps up? Does the candidate return the cup to the sink (or even gesture to do so)? Apparently, only around 10 percent of candidates return their cups. To Trent, this is a big indicator.

In the world of fine-dining kitchens, a saying was drummed into me: "Work clean, clean as you go—no clean, no go." I get the coffee cup test, I really do. I hate messy offices, clutter, and people who just don't clean up after themselves. It shows a lack of attention to detail and perhaps a lack of good manners.

But is this a true test of character? Does it really work? What happens if the person says, "No, I'm fine, thanks," and declines tea or coffee? These are questions for Trent.

A few months back, I found myself sitting with a group of eight people in the Four Seasons lobby in Las Vegas. No coffee cups in this story. As my group got up to leave where we were sitting, I moved a chair back to another table I'd borrowed it from (maybe instinct from my hospitality days). Another guest in my group said, "What are you doing? They have staff for that!" I was doing what I considered to be the right thing. Sometimes it's a small, polite gesture that demonstrates your character.

The Last Bite

———

"The only constant in life is change."
—HERACLITUS

I RECALL A MOMENT ON A LIVE TELEVISION BROADCAST that taught me an important lesson: When you're on air, be ready for anything. The host was recording from their studio while the program was recording the video of me at home in front of my computer camera. What I did not anticipate was that as I looked at the screen as the host was saying, "Nick Wyman, good morning, tell us about . . ." there was a tech failure, and instead of seeing the host who was interviewing me, I was seeing the video from the previous guest in his São Paulo hotel room. It seemed that the esteemed professor of economics had not closed his laptop, and his camera was still on. As the second question arrived, the professor stood up for a stretch to reveal shirt and tie above, tighty-whities below. No pants. Then, into the picture in her negligee came a woman I assumed was Mrs. esteemed professor.

There I was, full flight in the interview, trying to focus on the host's questions while staring at the professor in his very large white underwear and his wife conversing in their hotel room. What to do? Tell the studio? Look away? Press on? Maybe the audience was seeing me? I decided to push on. What choice did I have? Fortunately for them and myself, my face returned to the screen before anything further developed in the hotel room.

Thinking on your feet, adjusting to the current situation, is a skill. It's something you're taught in hospitality from day one. Adapt or perish, as they say. It also applied in my days in the kitchen when we ran out of food or spices and needed to adapt quickly.

Sometimes, the plan for success is simply not committing to a plan coming into the activity and having the courage to go for it, to be spontaneous, pivot, change your course, and stand by it, even if it means going against the grain. Adapt as you need to, but do something—pivot as necessary.

Life is not just a dress rehearsal, as they say. You are living the main show. Think back to inspirational people like Wik, whom we met earlier. He enjoys each day to its fullest. He believes, belongs, and contributes to his company and his family. And he is always present.

I hope you have seen the importance of strong leadership, especially recognizing that these have been turbulent times, and recognize more bumps are on the way.

As we wrap up, consider rethinking work strategies, particularly those for issues like hybrid work and meaningful work. Think about what engages employees, and use the uncertain times to connect or reconnect with people in your company and its culture.

I hope you enjoyed this read. In your own career, hustle hard, stay kind, and remain ambitious. And I would be remiss if I did not end with a food reference: let the world be your oyster.

Online Training Platforms — Elevating Your Teams

———

THIS APPENDIX LISTS A RANGE OF ONLINE TRAINING PLAT-forms designed to enhance the skills and knowledge of your workforce. From technical proficiencies to leadership training, these platforms offer a comprehensive suite of tools for businesses to cultivate a dynamic and well-equipped team. Take some time to explore them, or let your fingers do the walking—online.

Wide range of topics

- Coursera: Offers online courses and degrees from top universities and companies. https://www.coursera.org/
- edX: Offers online courses and degrees from top universities and companies. https://www.edx.org/
- Udemy: Offers online courses on a wide range of topics. https://www.udemy.com/

- Alison: Offers a wide range of free online courses on various topics, including business, IT, and health. https://alison.com/
- SkillShare: Offers specific real-life skill development topics. https://www.skillshare.com/

Software coding, technology, and data analytics

- Code.org: Offers STEM courses. https://code.org/
- Codecademy Pro: Provides in-depth coding learning experience with a focus on career readiness. https://www.codecademy.com/pro
- Udacity: Offers online courses and nanodegrees in IT, business, and data science topics. https://www.udacity.com/
- Treehouse: Offers online courses on coding, web design, and business topics. https://teamtreehouse.com/
- Skillcrush: Offers online courses on coding, design, and marketing. This platform has a strong focus on being inclusive. https://skillcrush.com/
- Pluralsight Flow: Provides analytics and insights to help teams improve their software development process. https://www.pluralsight.com/flow
- Plantoost: Offers a wide range of online courses on various topics, including tech, design, and business. https://www.plantoost.com/
- Google Digital Garage: Offers free online courses on digital marketing and other digital skills. https://learndigital.with-google.com/digitalgarage

Sales, marketing, design, and creative

- Skillcrush: Offers online courses on coding, design, and marketing. This platform has a strong focus on being inclusive. https://skillcrush.com/

- Plantoost: Offers a wide range of online courses on various topics, including tech, design, and business. https://www.plantoost.com/

- Udacity: Offers online courses and nanodegrees in IT, business, and data science topics. https://www.udacity.com/

- LinkedIn Learning: Offers online courses on marketing, design, and creative topics. https://www.linkedin.com/learning

- HubSpot Academy: Offers online courses on marketing, sales, and customer service. https://academy.hubspot.com/

- HubSpot Sales Hub: Provides training and courses on sales and customer service for businesses and organizations. https://www.hubspot.com/products/sales

- Adobe Creative Cloud: Offers online courses on creative software and tools. https://www.adobe.com/creativecloud

- Google Digital Garage: Offers free online courses on digital marketing and other digital skills. https://learndigital.with-google.com/digitalgarage

- Salesforce Trailhead: Offers online courses and training on the Salesforce platform and related topics. https://trailhead.salesforce.com/

- CreativeLive: Offers online courses on creative topics such as photography, art, marketing, business, and music. https://www.creativelive.com/

- Treehouse: Offers online courses on coding, web design, and business topics. https://teamtreehouse.com/
- Pluralsight: Offers online courses on technology, creative, and business topics. https://www.pluralsight.com/
- Marketing Artificial Intelligence Institute: Offers free and paid courses, webinars, in-person conferences, and a podcast about AI for marketers. https://www.marketingaiinstitute.com/

Business and technology

- LinkedIn Learning: Offers online courses on business, marketing, career, finance, creative, and technology topics. https://www.linkedin.com/learning
- LinkedIn Learning for Business: Offers courses and training solutions for businesses and organizations. https://www.linkedin.com/learning/business
- Udacity: Offers online courses and nanodegrees in IT, business, and data science topics. https://www.udacity.com/
- Skillsoft: Offers online courses and training solutions for businesses and organizations. https://www.skillsoft.com/
- edX for Business: Offers courses and training solutions for businesses and organizations. https://www.edx.org/business
- Treehouse: Offers online courses on coding, web design, and business topics. https://teamtreehouse.com/
- Pluralsight: Offers online courses on technology, creative, and business topics. https://www.pluralsight.com/
- Plantoost: Offers a wide range of online courses on various topics, including tech, design, and business. https://www.plantoost.com/

Foreign language learning

- Memrise: For foreign language courses. https://www.memrise.com/
- Duolingo: Popular for learning a new language with a gamified approach. https://www.duolingo.com/
- Babbel: Offers online courses for learning a new language with a focus on practical conversation skills. https://www.babbel.com/
- Rosetta Stone: Offers online language courses with a focus on immersive, real-life scenarios. https://www.rosettastone.com/
- International Language Exchange: Connect with learning partners anywhere in the world for mutual language practicing for free. https://en.language.exchange/

Learning management systems for in-house courses

- LearnDash: Provides a learning management system for businesses and organizations to create and distribute their own online courses. https://www.learndash.com/
- Udemy for Business: Provides a platform for companies to create and distribute their own online courses. https://www.udemy.com/business
- OpenSesame: Provides a platform for companies to create and distribute their own online courses and training. https://www.opensesame.com/
- Google Classroom: For basic business training. https://classroom.google.com/u/0

Governments and nonprofit organizations

- Coursera for Governments and Nonprofits: Provides courses and training solutions for government agencies and nonprofit organizations. https://www.coursera.org/government

Higher education

- LinkedIn Learning for Higher Education: Provides courses and training solutions for colleges and universities. https://www.linkedin.com/learning/higher-ed

- MIT OpenCourseWare: Provides free online courses and materials from the Massachusetts Institute of Technology. https://ocw.mit.edu/index.htm

- Open Learning Initiative: Provides free online courses and materials from Carnegie Mellon University. https://oli.cmu.edu/

- Stanford Online: Offers online courses and degrees from Stanford University. https://online.stanford.edu/

- Harvard Online Learning: Offers online courses and degrees from Harvard University. https://online-learning.harvard.edu/

- Yale Online: Offers online courses and degrees from Yale University. https://online.yale.edu/

- Academic Earth: Comprehensive platform for free online courses from top universities worldwide. Covers a diverse range of academic subjects. Ideal for lifelong learners, students, and educators. https://academicearth.org/

K–12 to early college

- Khan Academy: Popular for self-paced learning for skill mastery. Offers video tutorials on subjects including mathematics, science, reading, computing history, art history, economics, financial literacy, SAT, and MCAT. https://www.khanacademy.org/
- LessonPaths: For curating and sharing sequenced educational playlists or teaching plans. https://www.lessonpaths.com/

Specifically for people of color

- AfroTech University (Blavity): Offers educational resources and career development opportunities for Black students and professionals keen on entering the tech industry. https://afro-tech.com/university
- Management Leadership for Tomorrow (MLT): A national non-profit for transforming the leadership pipeline for under-represented communities, including Black, Latine, and Native American people. https://mlt.org/
- Black Business School: A low-cost alternative to college degrees for courses in small business, entrepreneurship, investing, wealth, and other topics. https://theblackbusinessschool.com/
- Code2040: A Black-led, national not-for-profit offering direct-service programs and pathways into the innovation economy for Black and Latine people. https://www.code2040.org/
- Latino Business Action Network: Partners with Stanford University to run a startup accelerator for Latine business owners and founders. https://www.lban.us/

For juniors

- Khan Academy Kids: Offers free online courses and materials for young children. https://www.khanacademy.org/kids
- Epic: Provides an online library of books and learning videos for kids. https://www.getepic.com/

Attributes

———

Happy

Creative   Focused   Hardworking

Determined   Helpful

Resourceful

Honest

Punctual   Clever   Compassionate

Friendly   Confident   Dependable

Diligent

Ambitious   Independent

Intuitive   Genuine   Loyal

Cooperative   Organized

Team Player   Capable

Notes

INTRODUCTION

1. World Economic Forum, "The Future of Jobs Report 2023," April 30, 2023, https://www.weforum.org/publications/the-future-of-jobs-report-2023/.

CHAPTER 1

1. Clayton M. Christensen, Michael E. Raynor, and Rory McDonald, "What Is Disruptive Innovation?" *Harvard Business Review*, December 2015, https://hbr.org/2015/12/what-is-disruptive-innovation.
2. John Wikstrom, personal email to the author.
3. John Wikstrom, personal email to the author.
4. *Becoming Warren Buffett*, directed by Peter W. Kunhardt and Brian Oakes, Home Box Office (HBO), 2017.
5. Marco Pierre White, *White Heat* (New York: Mitchell Beazley, 1990).

CHAPTER 2

1. Jorge Tamayo, Leila Doumi, Sagar Goel, Orsolya Kovács-Ondrejkovic, and Raffaella Sadun, "Reskilling in the Age of AI," *Harvard Business Review*, September–October 2023, https://hbr.org/2023/09/reskilling-in-the-age-of-ai?.
2. Daron Acemoglu and James Robinson, *Why Nations Fail: The Origins of Power, Prosperity, and Poverty* (New York: Crown Currency, 2013).
3. "Special Message to Congress on Urgent National Needs, 25 May 1961," White House Audio Collection, last updated October 28, 2023, https://www.jfklibrary.org/asset-viewer/archives/jfkwha-032.

CHAPTER 3

1. Patrice Weiss and Beverly Philip, "Lessons Learned: Using Teamwork as a Baseline to Navigate COVID-19," American Hospital Association, January 11, 2021, https://www.aha.org/news/headline/2021-01-11-lessons-learned-using-teamwork-baseline-navigate-covid-19.

2. Jamela Adams, "20 Companies That Offer Unlimited Vacation Days," *U.S. News & World Report*, May 10, 2024, https://money.usnews.com/careers/slideshows/companies-that-offer-unlimited-vacation-days.

CHAPTER 4

1. Mark McCrindle, "The Generations Defined," https://mccrindle.com.au/article/topic/demographics/the-generations-defined/.

2. Roberta Katz, Sarah Ogilvie, Jane Shaw, and Linda Woodhead, *Gen Z, Explained: The Art of Living in a Digital Age* (Chicago: University of Chicago Press, 2021), retrieved from https://press.uchicago.edu/ucp/books/book/chicago/G/bo115838546.html.

3. Mark McCrindle, "The Generations Defined."

CHAPTER 7

1. Håkan G. Lutz, personal communication with the author, November 30, 2023.

CHAPTER 8

1. Shawn Anchor, "The Happiness Dividend," *Harvard Business Review*, June 23, 2011, https://hbr.org/2011/06/the-happiness-dividend.

2. "Happy Workers Are 13% More Productive," University of Oxford, October 24, 2019, https://www.ox.ac.uk/news/2019-10-24-happy-workers-are-13-more-productive.

CHAPTER 9

1. "Nearly a Third of Employed Americans Have Not Received Any Formal Workplace Training from Their Current Employer," Ipsos, February 20, 2018, https://www.ipsos.com/en-us/news-polls/Nearly-a-Third-of-Employed-Americans-Have-Not-Received-Any-Formal-Workplace-Training-from-Current-Employer.

CHAPTER 10

1. Katja Grace, Harlan Stewart, Julia Fabienne Sandkühler, Stephen Thomas, Ben Weinstein-Raun, and Jan Brauner, "Thousands of AI Authors on the Future of AI," AI Impacts, April 2023, https://aiimpacts.org/wp-content/uploads/2023/04/Thousands_of_AI_authors_on_the_future_of_AI.pdf.

2. "Accelerating AI Skills: Preparing the Workforce for Jobs of the Future," Amazon Web Services (AWS) & Access Partnership, November 2023, https://assets.aboutamazon.com/e1/a0/17842ee148e8af9d55d10d75a213/aws-accelerating-ai-skills-us-en.pdf

CHAPTER 11

1. Jeffrey M. Jones, "U.S. Confidence in Higher Education Now Closely Divided," Gallup, July 8, 2024, https://news.gallup.com/poll/646880/confidence-higher-education-closely-divided.aspx.

2. "WSJ/NORC Poll March 2023," *Wall Street Journal*, March 2023, https://s.wsj.net/public/resources/documents/WSJ_NORC_ToplineMarc_2023.pdf.

3. Andrew Hanson, Carlo Salerno, Matt Sigelman, Mels de Zeeuw, and Stephen Moret, "Talent Disrupted: College Graduates, Underemployment, and the Way Forward," Burning Glass Institute, February 2022, https://www.burningglassinstitute.org/research/underemployment.

4. Sara Weissman, "Report: More Than Half of Recent 4-Year College Grads Are Underemployed," *Inside Higher Ed*, February 27, 2024, https://poetsandquantsforundergrads.com/news/report-more-than-half-of-recent-4-year-college-grads-are-underemployed.

5. Jon Marcus, "How Higher Education Lost Its Shine: Americans Are Rejecting College in Record Numbers, but the Reasons May Not Be What You Think," *The Hechinger Report*, August 10, 2022, https://hechingerreport.org/how-higher-education-lost-its-shine/.

CHAPTER 14

1. Stijn Van Nieuwerburgh, "The Remote Work Revolution: Impact on Real Estate Values and the Urban Environment," Working Paper 30662, National Bureau of Economic Research, November 2022, https://www.nber.org/system/files/working_papers/w30662/w30662.pdf .

2. "State of the Global Workforce: The Voice of the World's Employees," Gallup, 2023. https://www.gallup.com/workplace/349484/state-of-the-global-workplace-2023-report.aspx.

3. Kate Mogan and Delaney Nolan, "How Worker Surveillance Is Backfiring on Employers," BBC, January 30, 2023, https://www.bbc.com/worklife/article/20230127-how-worker-surveillance-is-backfiring-on-employers.

4. Morgan Smith, "Remote Workers Could Earn up to 30% More if They Come in to the Office 5 Days a Week, Research Shows," CNBC, March 27, 2024, https://www.cnbc.com/2024/03/27/remote-workers-get-up-to-30percent-pay-increase-for-switching-to-in-office-jobs-says-new-research.html.

5. Integrated Benefits Institute, "47% of Employees Say They'll Quit if Employer Orders Return to Office Full Time, According to Integrated Benefits Institute Analysis," PR Newswire, August 3, 2023, https://news.ibiweb.org/47-of-employees-say-theyll-quit-if-employer-orders-return-to-office-full-time-according-to-integrated-benefits-institute-analysis.

CHAPTER 16

1. "National Longitudinal Surveys," U.S. Bureau of Labor Statistics, https://www.bls.gov/nls/home.htm#anch41.

2. Tejas Vemparala, "Solving the Mystery of Millennial and Gen Z Job Hoppers," *Business News Daily*, October 24, 2023. https://www.businessnewsdaily.com/7012-millennial-job-hopping.html.

3. "Resign, Resigned, or Re-Signed? Millions of Pandemic-Era Job Quitters and Their Managers Wish They Had a Do-Over," UKG, April 2022, https://www.ukg.com/sites/default/files/legacy/ukg/media/files/Resign-Resigned-or-Re-Sign-Report-April-2022.pdf.

Index

About the Author

___

Photo credit: Hayden Brotchie Photography

NICHOLAS "NICK" WYMAN BEGAN HIS career as an award-winning chef, where he honed a unique blend of creativity and discipline. Transitioning from the culinary arts to the business world, Nick leveraged his leadership experience to become a globally recognized workforce practitioner. As the CEO of the Institute for Workplace Skills and Innovation Group (IWSI), he has been at the forefront of redefining career pathways, sparking a transformative shift in how the modern world views skills and success. Under his visionary leadership, IWSI has ignited more than 20,000 skills-based career paths, making a profound impact on both individuals and organizations worldwide. A leading authority on employment and talent development, Nick is the author of two influential books and a respected contributor to Forbes, Fast Company, the MIT Press journals, and CNBC.